TALKING
INDIAN

Other books by the author:

The Sacred: Ways of Knowledge, Sources of Life
The Sun Is Not Merciful
Ghost Singer
The Spirit of Native America

TALKING INDIAN

Reflections on Survival and Writing
ANNA LEE WALTERS

Firebrand
Books
Ithaca, New York

Book design by Besty Bayley
Cover design by Lee Tackett
Cover photograph by Monty Roessel
Typesetting by Bets Ltd.

Printed on acid-free paper in the United States by McNaughton &
Gunn

Library of Congress Cataloging-in-Publication Data

Walters, Anna Lee, 1946–
    Talking Indian: reflections on survival and writing / Anna Lee
Walters.
        p.   cm.
    Includes bibliographical references.
    ISBN 1-56341-022-2 (cloth) : ISBN 1-56341-021-4 (paper)
    1. Walters, Anna Lee, 1946–   .   2. Oto Indians—Biography.
3. Pawnee Indians—Biography.   4. Authors, Indian—Biography.
I. Title.
E99.O87W34   1992
818'.54—dc20
    [B]   92-27211
                                                                CIP

Acknowledgments

This material was written over a long period of time. I would like to thank the following people for their support and involvement in it: Herman Viola, Martha Royce Blaine and the late Garland Blaine, Andrea Loewenstein, Truman Dailey, Esther Gooden, Luther and Mae McGlaslin, Hilda Howell, and John and Roselyn Walters. Last of all I wish to thank Harry, Tony, and Daniel Walters for being the people they are.

This book is affectionately dedicated to Lena Arkeketa and Tom Hartico, both of whom no longer live, yet have never died. By the name Anna Lee Hartico, you will know me.

Contents

From Black Bear Creek

Part One
Oral Tradition

My first memories are not so much of *things* as as they are of *words* that gave shape and substance to my being and form to the world around me. Born into two tribal cultures which have existed for millennia without written languages, the spoken word held me in the mystical and intimate way it has touched others who come from similar societies whose literature is oral.

In such cultures, the spoken word is revered, and to it are attributed certain qualities. One quality is akin to magic or enchantment because the mystery of language and speech, and the processes of their development, as well as their origin, can never be fully explained. For the same reason, the spoken word is believed to be power which can create or destroy.

Members of nonliterate societies spend their lifetimes reaffirming that the spoken word lives of its own indescribable power and energy, floating apart and separate from individual human voices who utter it. Yet, paradoxically, we are also shown that it is through the power of speech, and the larger unified voice of oral tradition, that we exist as we do.

Listening is the first sense to develop in the womb. It is not surprising, then, that I was conscious of sounds earlier than anything else as an infant. Mainly, these were the sounds of the universe, the outdoors. They included whishing bird wings rising up into the sky, rustling trees, the cry of the mourning dove, and the rippling wind. They were the first nonhuman sounds I heard because my family spent most of the time outdoors. This awareness was followed by other sounds of life embracing me with deep sighs and measured breaths. Those human sounds then became syllables, or vocables, and voice patterns with intonations and inflections. Eventually and inexplicably they turned into words such as Waconda, meaning Creator, or the Great Mystery of Life, and *waduge,* meaning to eat, and Mayah, the Earth. Single words became explosions of sounds and images, and these traveled outward in strings of sentences or melodies and songs.

There were many individual voices, male and female, old and young, scattered about me, and these voices expressed themselves in two languages, Otoe and English. Some of the people were literate in English. Otoe was unwritten for the most part. But more often than not, as if by some magnetic pull of oral tradition, the individual tribal voices unconsciously blended together, like braided strands of thread, into *one* voice, story, song, or prayer. That thread stretched, unbroken, to a pre-time and origin that still lived in the mystery and power of the Otoe language, their *spoken* word, even translated into English as it had been for well over a century before I was born. The echo of that tribal voice, in Otoe or English, never disappears or fades from my ear, not even in the longest silences of the people, or in my absences from them.

In the Pawnee culture, the experience with that language and their spoken word, and their numerous voices flowing into one, was identical to the Otoe experience, though Pawnee culture and language are distinctly different because the two tribes are unrelated. The Pawnees had also adopted English to a certain extent by the time I was born. But before that, daring Frenchmen and Spaniards had mingled among them and intermarried with them, thereby introducing those languages. French and Spanish intermarriage had also occurred among the Otoe, but even with these influences, as well as those of other tribal cultures through adoption and intermarriage, the Pawnees and the Otoes retained their own unique voices, their own memories, consciousness, and spirits. In their approaches to the world, reality, and existence, and through the spoken word, they were alike. They both had extended a pattern of life over countless generations, through the centuries, and credited their survival and continuity to the power of their oral traditions. These are haunting and powerful voices that still recall prehistoric tribal visions and experiences that are the core of their identities today.

The Otoe voice seemed to originate and drift from the north, much further away from Oklahoma where the Otoes then resided. Nevertheless, I was able to hear it when I was alone in the cotton fields north of my grandparents' house. It whispered of a time before Indian Territory, before the Oklahoma hills where I was born, and I'm certain, too, that this was the same voice of a relative who retold old stories with a new twist. He often sat at our table speaking to us in whispers, and occasionally in shouts from across the fields, of the life, history, and fate that we all shared as one tribal people.

Most of the time, the Otoe voice was as fluid as the water from which we were told that we came. In water we were conceived, and we made our first appearance on its shorelines in clans of totem beings who have since not ceased to be. The clans of Bear, Elk, Buffalo, and others traveled in circles for a while, leaving their prints deeply impressed in the mud. Their totem voices swirled visibly overhead in the immenseness of the universe, and this is how the clans knew they lived. Silence and speech at the water's edge alternated here. Remember that we need both, we are told. The totem voices took turns speaking—the Bears roared, the Eagles screeched, the Pigeons cooed—until all the clans had spoken. Silence followed. *Silence.* Then all the totem beings spoke at once. Yes, through their speech and voices, and through the ensuing silence, the people, the clans, knew they lived. This is the power of language, but often it is not realized until silence prevails. Silence. *Remember both, we are told.*

It is understandable that the Otoe voice did pause from time to time. In its place silence reigned, and in these periods, other affirmations about the universe and life were absorbed through the other senses. These affirmations always seemed to correspond to oral tradition. Then the Otoe tribal voice began again, sometimes at the periphery of my world, and other times it seemed to come from deep inside *me*. Later when I began to write, it is what I drew upon.

Today, there are seven surviving clans in the tribe. These are the Bear, Beaver, Elk, Eagle, Buffalo, Pigeon, and Owl. The story that follows is one of the many versions that describes the origin of these clans. Within the respective clans, details of clan behavior are told in greater depth and are often known only to the members of the clan. This is one of the hereditary "rights" of a clansman.

Nothing existed at the beginning except an abundance of water. It flowed everywhere, eventually pushing all life out of it. In time, the water receded and land surfaced. Vegetation sprouted. Forests reached towering heights. In the recesses of forests, animals and birds dwelt. All life spoke the same language.

From the life-giving waters, the Bear Clan rose and came ashore. They peered about the dry world and thought they were the first people here. But they were quickly disappointed when they found the tracks of others embedded in the soft mud, leading out and away from the water. Following these signs, the Bear Clan chased the Beaver Clan, whom they eventually caught. The Beaver Clan, a diplomatic people, suggested that the clans become brothers and live together in harmony because alone, life was so hard. The intent of the Bear Clan was to kill the Beaver Clan when they found them, but the Bears were soon pacified by their new kin and resigned themselves to the fact that they were not the first people. So the Bear and Beaver Clans kept each other company and were companions at The Beginning. Some time passed before the Bear and Beaver clans met other peoples, and the two were content to think no others

*existed. Then it happened that the Bear and Beaver Clans
came upon the Elks, whom they desired to kill. But instead
the Elks proposed that they be allowed to accompany the
two clans. After a time, the Bear and Beaver Clans had a
change of heart and agreed that all could be brothers and
help one another.*

*Now the sky people came through the sky opening and
swooped down to earth, where they found evidence of three
other clans. The Eagles knew that there were more people
in the other three clans than in the Eagle Clan. The Eagles
approached the three clans to join them, and once more the
number of clans grew. Having decided to live together, they
began sharing among themselves certain things and knowledge that had before belonged solely to the individual clans.
This was now used to help all of the clans.*

*In order to learn how to live, the clans called upon
Waconda, the Creator. Waconda taught each clan certain
things and gave each group certain sacred knowledge and,
therefore, rights associated with a sacred pipe that also was
a gift from Waconda. In this manner (of the sacred pipe)
the four clans lived.*

*In time, the Bear, Beaver, Elk, and Eagle Clans met
the Snake, Buffalohead, Owl, and Pigeon Clans. The last
two, like the Eagles, were from the sky. The Buffalohead (re-
named Buffalo), Owl, Pigeon, and Snake (now extinct) had
their own pipe, and this sacred possession they offered to
the Bear, Beaver, Elk, and Eagle Clans. At first, this gesture was ignored by the Bears and the pipe was rejected.
But the Bears softened, and finally Bear, Beaver, Elk, and
Eagle Clans accepted the pipe which was an offering of
friendship and coexistence. They reciprocated, making a
similar gesture of friendship. So it was in these acts that
everything began.*[1]

Often the Otoe voice of oral tradition has no human gender in my ears, for it reflects a universal community on earth and in the sky that includes the fish, plants, animals, and birds with which the world is shared. Voices of that community are very much intertwined with Otoe oral tradition, and perhaps this is why it is as expansive and ethereal as it is.

Masculine and feminine are layered into it all, indefinable and inseparable in coalescence. In my writing, the voice of oral tradition is both male and female. The character Old Man in the short story, "The Sun Is Not Merciful," says the same things as more formal tribal oral tradition.

Old Man said, "Girls, we're fishermen from way back yonder, way back when time first began. Fact is, alla us came outta water. Happened up north, round Canada somewhere. Well, girls, we found ourselves on the shore of this wide lake. We came outta it, see? Weren't no other people then—just us back then. And that's why we're fishermen from way back, fore time even began."

"How'd we get here?" Lydia asked Old Man when she was going on seven years. Bertha and she waited for Old Man's reply as they washed pearly white shells in the warm creek water.

"We walked," Old Man said. "Damn near walked all over this old earth. First we walked from way up north, wandered around a bit for a few years, trying to get our bearings ah guess. Then we began to drift southward. Groups of people got tired of wandering around all the time, so they began to drop off, break away and settle down. But us, we weren't tired. We kept on the move, following rivers and creekbeds till we finally stopped along a river in Nebraska. Know where that is? It's up north, bout a four-week walk from here. Anyway, we stayed in Nebraska another hunnerd years and more. Then some strangers came, came close enough to walk through the midst of us. To make a long story short, we up and left Nebraska not long after that. Came down here on *foot with our food and clothing carried on covered wagons and pack animals. Ah remember that, ah made the trip myself. Was a little fellar near your age. Yes sir, recollect that. We walked for nearly four weeks to get down here.''*[2]

My women characters are unusually strong because they are modeled after Otoe and Pawnee women. But physical strength and aggressiveness do not make them who and what they are. That identity comes from the integrity of what they have been told about the universe and their place in it. This is seen in a counterpart to Old Man, his daughter Lydia, in the same story.

"See this lake, the deep water. That's what calls us here. We fisherpeople, Hollis. Fished since time began. We came up outta water, water that looked pretty much like this here. My heart is in the water Hollis. Can't be drowned, Hollis. We bound to keep coming back, Hollis. Have to, there's no other way."[3]

Lydia reaffirms what Old Man is and says they both are. In effect, she mirrors him, though he is male and she is not. Oral traditions are always consistent. If they were not, they could not be trusted, much like the idea of a deceptive narrator.

In the story called "The Resurrection of John Stink,"[4] I relied heavily on informal oral stories about John Stink, someone who actually lived in the early part of this century. Tall tales grew up around him in a wonderful way. The narrator in the story is an embodiment of oral tradition.

My mother inspired the creation of this story, which is an entirely fictitious look at a remarkable man and legendary character among the Oklahoma tribes, much as Jesse James or Billy the Kid of the Old West are to the larger society. These figures trigger many fanciful tales incorporating historical fact and information. When it comes to John Stink, however, my mother's stories are the only ones I ever heard about him.

The Pawnee voice of oral tradition has always been more formal than the Otoe's to my ear, and a male element does seem more dominant. The voice emanates from several directions. If it could be seen, it would be a glow of amber light that always dimly pulsates on the darkest night, visible from immeasurable distances only by an eye that knows what to seek.

Pursuing the voice has led me to Old Mexico, and the American Southwest, and across the swampy Southeast, as well as toward the Plains in the far north and back down to Oklahoma again. In times past, the Pawnees roamed these places. The voice describes all of them. *The ground was hard and mean,* it said of the rocky Southwest. Of the fertile green valleys of Nebraska it spoke of sacred places where certain spirit beings and animals could be reached. Thus, the voice leads the Pawnee people about, to other times and places, as far out as into the heavens and up to the stars, a journey still accessible, but only through the spoken word of Pani Pakuru, the Pawnee language.

We envision Pawnee life throughout time as it describes the people, their prehistory and history, and their ceremonies, and repeats ancient prayers and songs. The voice speaks and we listen. It is our voice and the voice of our ancestors, and yet it is something more, something larger. We cannot separate ourselves from it because it is impossible to know where it ends and we begin. In silence and wonder, I write down details of growing up in this flow, trying to capture the pauses of the people and their words, and the necessary silences needed to fully comprehend all of this.

> *Sister and I were little, and Uncle Ralph came to visit us. He lifted us over his head and shook us around him like gourd rattles. He was Momma's younger brother, and he could have disciplined us if he desired. That was part of our custom. But he never did. Instead, he taught us Pawnee words. "Pari is Pawnee and pita is man," he said. Between the words he tapped out drumbeats with his fingers on the*

table top, ghost dance and round dance songs that he sud-
denly remembered and sang. His melodic voice lifted over
us and hung around the corners of the house for days. His
stories of life and death were fierce and gentle. Warriors
dangled in delicate balance.

He told us his version of the story of Pahukatawa, a
Skidi Pawnee warrior. He was killed by the Sioux, but the
animals, feeling compassion for him, brought Pahukatawa
to life again. "The Evening Star and the Morning Star bore
children, and some people say that these offspring are who
we are," he often said. At times he pointed to those stars
and greeted them by their Pawnee names. He liked to pray.
He prayed for Sister and me, for everyone and every tiny
thing in the world, but we never heard him ask for anything
for himself from Atius, the Father. [5]

The information imparted by Uncle Ralph to the girls in this story
leads not only backward in time but *forward* as well. Oral tradition
does that too, extends into both past and future. The voice of oral tradition endures because its teachings reconcile and connect different
periods and generations in a very cohesive way by focusing on larger
tribal vision and experience. It includes cosmology and worship.

Each tribe has a particular way of worship, although this has not
been recognized historically by those outside Native societies. Prayers
are part of oral tradition because their procedures, and frequently the
wording itself, are memorized and handed down to the next generation without written records. The praying voice of oral tradition is very
formal and precise. It calls out sacred names of tribal deities, ancestors, and guardians. Both the Pawnees and the Otoes expect acknowledgment of this practice from the tribal dieties. If this had not
been consistently received throughout the tribes' existence, they would
not have continued to pray in this way, even as they do today.

Prayer employs repetition, ritual, drama, and reverence in its recitation and formulation. "Waconda," it says in Otoe, Great Mystery,
meaning that vital thing or phenomenon in life that cannot ever be en-

tirely comprehensible to us. What is understood, though, through the spoken word, is that silence is also Waconda, as is the universe and *everything* that exists, tangible and intangible, because none of these things are separate from that life force. It is all Waconda, and being what it is and what we are, the Otoes speak to it and communicate with it uniquely when using their own tongue.

In the short story "The Devil and Sister Lena," Lena talks about this understanding of the universe, its holy nature, and how her people interact with it.

> *The preacher became more confident then and boldly said, "I hear you people don't have religion. Don't believe in God or Jesus."*
>
> *For the first time in their conversation, Lena's mouth clamped shut. Her lips pursed tightly. She looked at him with open distrust and sat down again on the makeshift chair. . . . "I'll tell you what I can. We don't got Jesus. We got something else. It's every thing. Hard to sit and talk about it. Can't say it in so many words. So we sing, we dance. What we have is a mystery. Don't got answers for it and don't understand it. But it's all right. Jest live right in it. Side by side."*[6]

Lena passes on this same information to her grandchild, but in a more loving and tender way. She says:

> *"Out there, they's a lot what lives and moves. Us peoples knows it because it touches us. Then us peoples seems like little things next to it. It big and mysterious. Yes, lotsa times us peoples feel it, if we want to or not. It jest touches us, and us peoples thinks we's part of it. . . . That's how come we knows they's other things in the world sides only what we see. Us peoples been thinking this since the first day. Don't hardly talk bout it much tween ourselves. Can't say much bout something what's plain as day. But you jest a*

*baby, so I tole you. Gonna help you out a little so you can
go a long ways.''*[7]

In this way, the grandchild in the story learns, as many children
in tribal societies still learn, as I learned from the instructive voice
of oral tradition.

When the voice sings, as it is prone to do, songs are often given
the same formality as prayers, although many songs are not about dieties. Songs recognize individuals, or deeds, or particular emotions:
love, grief, and joy. They are sometimes very profound, such as the
one that follows:

> *I do not understand as I live. I do not understand as I live.
> Make thoughts for me. I do not understand as I live.* (Free
> translation.)

This was translated by the late Garland Blaine. He interpreted the song
in this way:

> *The meaning of my life is unclear to me. The meaning of
> my life is unclear to me. Give me a blessing (i.e. help me
> to understand). The meaning of my life is unclear to me.*

In many tribes songs are still not written down, and it is frowned
upon to record them as a way of learning the songs. Some tribes have
hundreds of songs known only by them, and new ones are still being
composed in tribal languages, or English, or both.

The Otoe and Pawnee voices of oral tradition have never been
steady monotones. They lilt and dip, rise and fall, and have rhythms
and characters of their own that are separate from those of individual
tribal members. They are the words of all those who have gone before us. *Listen to this,* more formal oral tradition says. *This is where
everything began. This is where these words began. This is where creation began. This is where time began. This is where the people began.* Its vitality and force is what gives it a life of its own. It is differ-

ent from any individual human voice because it spans infinite time and life. It is an ancient being, this voice that survives longer than one human being ever will.

Neither is the voice of oral tradition always so formal. It expresses derision, humor, irreverence, and other emotions that all generations have experienced. But its expression of these experiences are more aloof and objective than an individual human response would be in an exact or similar circumstance. It lends perspective and tolerance to everyday events.

This distance is felt and seen in "The Resurrection of John Stink." Briefly, in the story, John Stink is an outcast in his society. He is accidentally buried by the only friend he has in the world. After several days, he becomes conscious in his grave, and his rescue is accomplished in a rather memorable way. But he does not enjoy a resurrection of love and compassion from his people; his life is one of further rejection. They barely tolerate him, and they balance this stingy tolerance with biting humor about the name with which they reward him after his escape from death. The narrator says:

> John Stink's first appearance in town after that caused a commotion. The people whispered loudly, detesting him more than ever because of his resurrection.
>
> It was then that they began to call him John Stink. They laughed among themselves, pleased with the name they gave him. They said that the dead did stink after a while, and he stunk most of all.[8]

There had already been numerous John Stink stories before I heard my first one about him. The name John Stink, in itself, was so memorable, and the stories of him so incredible and varied, that I thought of my tale as simply another in the tradition of John Stink storytellers—except that mine was *written* as fiction. In other words, I made most of it up!

Oral tradition has influenced my writing in all the ways I have described. But this has not been the only tribal influence. Another was also exerted by my early teachers. This is why my first memories are not so much of things as they are of words sung by one old man to a child of three or four. He sang in Otoe, pounding an imaginary drum in his hand as an accompaniment to his song while the child danced in circles around his feet. She danced as she had seen her grandmother dance. Years later, I wrote of his words:

Grandpa, I saw you die in the Indian hospital at Pawnee, twenty years ago, but look who is talking. You know of it all too well.

I can measure time. You, yourself, showed me how. But how does one count another man's loss? Do I count on my fingers the memories and think of the stars as my tears?

Grandpa, beautiful brown, old Otoe!
At Red Rock, do you still cross the creek
to walk your rolling green hills?
Has time with her sense of duty
covered your tracks with mine?

Then let me climb the hills for you.
My children shall follow me with theirs after them. One day we will be so many that we could hold hands, form a circle and dance around the earth.

Grandpa, to you I close my eyes from distractions and open my heart.
Remember when I was a rabbit?
It was the manner of a child who knew nothing but play. You could not be but what you were, a handsome but tired powerful old bear.

I say you and know this to be true.
You would pull yourself upright and scan my horizon, hands up as though you would advise me some caution. In the early morning sun, I saw it circle you with its brilliance.

*It seemed to me to be a sign. Then down, you relaxed, sig-
naling me with your spirit. Rabbit, be happy, go with the
morning!*

*Grandpa, I saw an old bear hold a rabbit
ever so gently in one huge hand.
I heard him sing bear words rabbit didn't know
but could understand.
The bear was sleepy. The rabbit could tell
because the bear would often yawn.*

*Grandpa, the bear would then speak.
This is what he said, "Rabbits are fond of songs that sing
    about fried bread!"*

*Old bear gave the song to the rabbit.
They held it between them to make it strong
with laughter from the rabbit and the bear.
There is not another one like it.
My children have searched for one.
I brought the song here now so you can look at it.
We will sing it!*

*Grandpa, old bear has passed away but the rabbit remains.
For four nights old bear lay alone very cold, silently greeting
people who came to warm him with their words.
All for you they drummed and sang in Otoe.
It was to tell the people of the world that it would be wise
to mourn as we were one less, and therefore not as strong.*

*On the fourth day, old bear left the rabbit far behind. He
began a lonely journey for which he was in no hurry but was
the next in line.
All the people gathered to bring old bear tears that pale day.
It made a simple rabbit very proud when you gracefully accepted them in the old way.*

Grandpa, I see the rabbit now and then, in a water mirror.

He comes and goes.
Years have shaped a bear around a jumpy rabbit.
The bear sings. I know it. Within himself, he sings of rab-
bits and fried bread.

Grandpa, I tell you this. It comes from memories of long
ago. It was something that you said. [9]

Grandpa, I tell you this. It comes from memories of long ago. It
was something that you said.

There was another person, a woman, who was always present beside the old man, at the very beginning. It was these two people who
taught me about the power and meaning of words.

The grandfather who reared me was born in Nebraska. That was
one of the words taught and repeated to their offspring: Ni-bra-th-ka,
with a trill over the *r,* is an Otoe word meaning Flat or Shallow Water. The old man was born there about 1873 to a father whose name
was Har-ti-coo, meaning Go Back. His mother was young, about
twenty, and his father was much older. It is also said that the old man,
my grandfather, was orphaned when he was young.

When the Otoes were relocated from Nebraska to Indian Territory in 1881, this is the story he told of the removal, his summary of
what happened to the Otoes on their journey to Indian Territory and
what it all meant:

> *"The people walked. They walked down here. During*
> *the walk, something extraordinary happened. In Nebraska,*
> *the tribe had a number of dogs. When it came time for the*
> *people to move, they decided to leave these animals behind.*
> *There were too many to transport and to care for. As the peo-*
> *ple packed their wagons and prepared to depart, the dogs*
> *followed them everywhere. But our people shooed them*
> *away and even threw objects at them, hoping the dogs would*
> *leave the villages on their own. After such treatment some*
> *of the dogs did disappear into the Nebraska landscape. Then*

*it was time for the people to abandon the villages them-
selves. They took one last look back and they saw the sil-
houettes of the dogs, their tails wagging, as they whined after
the people. As the people traveled, occasionally one or two
dogs made their way into camp, and the people chased them
away again. But every now and then, the people heard bark-
ing in the distance. Finally the dogs were seen and heard
no more. The landscape became quiet, except for the movement of the people and their conversations among themselves. Days passed.*

*About four weeks later the people arrived in Indian Ter-
ritory, uncertain of what the future held for them. They set
up camps along a winding creek and began to unpack. Not
too long after, a few days perhaps, packs of dogs limped into
camp, seeking out old masters.''* (A retelling.)

The old man said that the dogs were skinny and their paws were
sore. Though he never said it himself, he was touched by this extraordinary behavior. Often there was silence after he spoke. Silence. It
was the only appropriate response to what he said, his unending story.

His spouse, my paternal grandmother, was the consummate storyteller. She understood stories, words *and* silence. She was born in 1884
and her father was the acting head chief of the Otoe-Missouria Tribe
between 1881 and 1896. Perhaps no one has taken her place as the
supremely skilled storyteller and tribal woman she was. It was through
her words that she lived as she did, touching the other dimensions of
the universe in a verbal and mystical way. In my writing, I have molded
several characters and stories after her, her words and her actions.

But for their words, these two figures would not have been so
grand or alive. The old man died before I was ten. It is rather miraculous that I have retained most of what I knew of him, especially con-
sidering the gaps of recollection I was to experience later growing up
without him. My grandmother died when I was a teenager.

No, I do not remember things so much as words from my earlier
years, and this characteristic has always been with me. Memory of

words is the source of all my writing. The spoken word has therefore played a major part in my life as a writer and tribal person. It set me on a mystical journey to its source that I have pursued my whole life. Profound respect for the integrity and complexity of oral tradition has been consistently reaffirmed all along the way. To trust the power and vitality of my own words as they leave me and float out into the universe, and to respect my own voice as much as I do the voices of other creatures in the universe, are perhaps the greatest lessons of writing and survival that I have learned thus far.

Notes:

1. From *The Otoe-Missouria Elders: Centennial Memoirs* (Otoe-Missouria Tribe, 1981).

2. All of the stories excerpted by Anna Lee Walters are from *The Sun Is Not Merciful* (Ithaca, New York: Firebrand Books, 1985). "The Sun Is Not Merciful," pp. 116-117.

3. p. 132.

4. "The Resurrection of John Stink."

5. "The Warriors," p. 12.

6. "The Devil and Sister Lena," p. 67.

7. p. 70.

8. "The Resurrection of John Stink," p. 61.

9. "Hartico" in *The Third Woman: Minority Women Writers of the United States*, ed. Dexter Fisher (Boston: Houghton-Mifflin, 1980), pp. 110-112.

Talking Indian

"Night is the best time for learning," the hundred-year-old man told his visitor. "It's a good teacher." They sat under tall swaying trees that leaned over them and blew soft moist whispers in their ears. The earth and sky were one then, shimmering in a pulsating glow from the translucent moon and stars. In the flat violet forest, quick-silver coyotes sang. Their songs rose like silver threads above the trees and disappeared into the flickering stars. Just then, the white dog at their feet lifted its head out of the darkness to lick the old man's hand with a warm pink tongue. Afterward, it lay back down and melted into the ground again.

The old man kept his voice low out of respect to the darkness. "You came here for a reason. What might that be?"

His visitor didn't answer but sat like a sculpted statue to his right. The visitor had been like that for over an hour by the old man's time. "You are longing for something," he continued. "You hunger for it but you can't name it because you don't know what it is. You have searched for it everywhere. . .in money, in drink, and what else? You really have tried everything to find it, haven't you?"

He looked at the statue in the moonlight, searching for its eyes, but they were empty spaces in its face. The statue looked heavier and bulkier then. The coyotes played closer, still yapping at the twinkling stars.

"It's for the old stories and songs that you grieve," he said. "That's what you want and need."

The head of the statue then pivoted slowly toward him. Its large eyes were dull abalone moons. They stared distantly into space.

"You came all the way back here for a story. You came all the way back to hear someone, anyone, talking Indian, didn't you?" he asked.

The eyes in the statue closed, the head turned away again. He heard a long sigh in the trees, and then a sniffle.

"For what you are searching is right here," he told the unmoving statue. "This will give you life." He noted the statue's heaviness again. "You were right to come back."

The trees bent low and blew on the old man and his visitor. A few minutes passed in the rustle of the wind before he spoke again. When he did, it wasn't in English.

He said, "It is important and curious to remember that everything we two-leggeds know about being human, we learned from the four-leggeds, the animals and birds, and everything else in the universe. None of this knowledge is solely our own."

He laughed at what he had just said, and a night hawk answered him.

The head of the statue pivoted toward him a second time. The abalone moons glistened momentarily and then became dull again.

"Everything we are was taught us, you see? This is what the stories are, the teachings of who we are."

The eyes of the statue began to gleam. Its head tilted toward him.

"That's why we need the stories. Without them we grieve. For ourselves, for direction, for meaning."

The statue still sat in the same way, listening to his voice weaving in and out of the dusky trees, the luminous stars, and the vibrant night.

"All these creatures and beings out here talk," the old man said, and motioned to the forest. "Even today. They told our elders a lot."

The coyotes had grown silent to hear the old man, but they had left their silver threads in the sky.

The head of the statue turned jerkily toward the violet forest, it lifted its abalone eyes to the sky, and then they settled on the old man once more, glowing with an internal light.

The old man laughed when he saw the abalone moons come to life.

The hands of the statue lifted and dropped again.

"What is it?" he asked.

The statue finally spoke. "I can't understand a word you're saying," it said. "I think I remember those sounds though." The voice was doubtful. "Will you speak English?"

The old man shook his head no as firmly as the trees shook around him. He continued talking Indian. "I speak the language of the universe. This is the same language spoken out there." He thrust his lips forward.

"Listen," he said.

The trees swung their branches down, leaves rustled everywhere. Animals rushed through the violet night. The dog at their feet yawned and stretched. Water trickled over colored rocks and down the creek in the distance. Iridescent dust rose in a swirl, spinning through the forest and woods before it settled.

The bulkiness of the stony statue fell away in the shimmering moonlight. Its eyes stared at the old man, and its head loosened and bent forward. The old man could feel what was happening.

His visitor wiped her eyes, using the sleeves of her long shirt.

"I remember!" she said in a whisper.

He didn't ask what she remembered. He waited, listening carefully to the sounds of the night. Almost two hours passed. During that time she blew her nose often and tried to speak, but nothing ever came out.

Finally, she calmed again and said, "They wouldn't ever let me speak it, you know. Don't talk Indian, they always said. Later, when I grew up, that's what I said to my own children, too. How could this have happened? Will you teach me to talk Indian all over again?" she asked.

He nodded, admiring her abalone eyes. "As long as I am here, but don't forget that this is still the best teacher." His finger encircled everything around them.

Later, they walked toward her vehicle. The dog followed, a brush against his leg. He looked down at it, the outline on the ground, and heard a soft panting sound. "This animal here feels very protective toward me," he said. "This is the one animal that's still the closest to human beings after all that we've done to them." His visitor paused and listened for the yapping of quick, silver coyotes again.

"A long time ago, two-leggeds and four-leggeds were just as close as we are with dogs today. Of course, in those days two-leggeds were close to all of nature and a trust existed between the two-leggeds and the four-leggeds." His visitor took his arm and held onto him when the dog let out a little growl and darted off into the glowing night.

"Two-leggeds were permitted to hunt and stalk four-leggeds, if they followed the procedure given them by the four-leggeds is what the stories say." The dog returned, a metallic flash in the night.

"For hundreds of years, this is how it was. The two-leggeds honored the trust."

"Then, another kind of two-legged creature appeared on the scene. He didn't talk or do anything like us. He brought with him an unfamiliar weapon. It produced a shattering, popping, cracking sound. The four-leggeds had never heard anything like that before. That sound was what broke the trust, the relationship between the two. Never would the four-leggeds permit two-leggeds that close to them again." The dog at their feet nudged the leg of the visitor as she climbed into her car. The old man wasn't through, old storyteller that he was.

"But old folks always say that the distance between two-leggeds and four-leggeds nowadays hasn't changed four-leggeds in any way. The distance has only changed us two-leggeds, made us worse off, more pitiful. They say that the four-leggeds still talk the way they always have. It's we who've forgotten how to listen. I guess we lost a lot when we quit talking Indian."

* * *

Not even when Eddie gave Maxine an early morning kiss as he left for the day did she wake. By the time she opened her eyes, it was midday and the house was too warm. She crawled out of bed and stared at herself in the bathroom mirror before rinsing her face in cold water. She raised the windows a couple of inches in each room and went to nibble on anything she could find in the refrigerator. A list of things to do today hung from a magnetic hook on the refrigerator door. Still in dark blue pajamas and barefoot, she balanced a jar of grape jelly, a burnt piece of toast, and a stick of margarine on a saucer in one hand, and a coffee cup in the other, moving toward the kitchen table. Then she found a newspaper, a couple of days old, and some back issues of popular magazines to which she could devote her full attention. She was always behind on the latest national news and on fashion, but it never affected what happened with those anyway.

She looked around the room. Granted it was chaotic, but not dirty. The house was quiet and peaceful, with only the sound of the wind slipping in through the open windows. The clock on the wall above the table ticked loudly toward noon, but she ignored it. She would not hurry today to complete the housework that would always be there, or even to comb her hair. She ate leisurely and read the paper and magazines thoroughly. When she accidentally poured a lukewarm cup of coffee on her pajamas because she was too engrossed in reading, she became aware of the ticking clock again and the waiting list hanging on the refrigerator door.

She decided to start the housework in the bedroom, leaving the kitchen table as it was for now, covered with crumbs and spilled coffee. She dabbed the stain on her pajamas with a kitchen towel and stood at the window, above the sink, looking out. It was a bright and warm day, but a strong wind gusted past the window. Scraps of paper flew by and dropped to the ground. Other than this whirlwind, nothing happened out there. The neighborhood was quiet. All the children had climbed aboard their school buses even before Eddie had left. At the next house, an older woman cleaned the yard, fighting the wind.

Maxine looked up at the poplar tree she and Eddie had planted sometime earlier. It had grown as tall as the roof, and it swayed in the breeze. Its leaves glistened and shook. The tree cast a cool, moving violet shadow on the ground and on the window, an animated shadow that moved all over the side of the house and around the base of the tree. The tree tempted her to forget her housework and go outside and recline under it for a while. She wanted to hear its leaves rustle in the breeze, but she let the temptation pass and went to the bedroom instead.

She turned on the television set, adjusted the horrible pink and green tints, and put the volume on low. She pulled the window shade down and let it snap up, filling the room with soft light. On this side of the house, at this window, the street had no traffic. Pedestrians were usually few. She began to pull off bedding, blankets, sheets, and pillowcases. These she carried to the washing machine on the back porch and stuffed them inside. She added a cup of detergent to the washer, but didn't turn it on. She went back to the bedroom where she rolled up all four rugs on the floor and set these outside the bedroom door. Then she cleaned the dresser tops, wiped the mirror with window cleaner, and even sprayed the TV glass with it. Before she put the glass cleaner away, she squirted a foamy circle on the window. She wiped the window in sweeping circular motions and inspected it carefully when she was done. Then she looked outside again. The tree across the street shimmied in a gusty wind. Blue jays tried to lift off the ground. A couple of stray dogs stood in the corner of the yard. She didn't pay any attention to them. She turned away and went to work again.

She picked everything off the floor, from under the bed, and around it. There were magazines, shoes, boots, and clothing in her arms when she was through. These she put in a jumble on the bed before putting each one away in its proper place. Her reflection went in and out of the mirror as she passed it walking back and forth. A light spray of fine dust flew in the window and sprinkled the floor.

She struggled to turn the mattress over, fighting with it for five minutes before she finally succeeded. Her pajamas were torn in her effort, and her hair hung down her face in loose ringlets. She pushed them back and went for a broom.

The room smelled of furniture polish, and she did too. She sniffed at her hands and at the lemon scent on her pajamas. She moved the bed away from the wall and swept in the empty space before pushing the bed back again. She brushed the dust off the sill and started to close the window, but it was calm outside then, no wind bending the trees. She left it open and felt the warm breeze stir the room. The strange dogs still sat at the edge of the yard, facing away from her. One was dark red and the other light brown.

After she swept the room, she filled a plastic bucket with sudsy water and dipped an old mop into it. The mop handle had splinters where the paint had flaked off from so much use. As she picked a splinter out of her hand, she lifted her head and stood motionless for a second. Had she heard someone outside? She waited, but the people in the soap opera were all that could be heard. She took the mop in hand and began to push it under the bed. She stopped a second time, stood motionless, and stared at the window, listening. On television, a fair young man with long fluttering lashes declared his undying love to a young woman confined to a hospital bed. He leaned over to embrace her. A nurse stood beside them, eavesdropping on their conversation. A close-up of the nurse's face revealed tears rolling down it, tinged with midnight blue mascara.

Maxine turned the volume all the way down and started mopping. Voices drifted to her again. She stopped what she was doing and looked at the television picture. The patient in the bed was talking to her sweetheart. Her lips moved soundlessly. In the next scene, her sweetheart and the nurse stood in the hall outside the room. The fair young man then held the nurse's hand, caressing it suggestively. Maxine couldn't hear anything. She went back to work.

Voices entered the room again, this time much clearer. People were outside. She glanced at herself in the mirror. She looked dreadful. Quickly, she hid the mop and bucket on the back porch and went into the bathroom to find a hairbrush. The voices were gone when she returned. She walked to the window and looked out. No one was around at all. Puzzled, she turned the TV off and brushed her hair vigorously, pinning it up, just so. She put a dab of Vaseline on her lips.

As she peeled off her pajama top, she heard the voices once more. They were very clear. She leaned toward them, nude to the waist, frozen momentarily, straining to hear. One voice was male and the other was female. She ran to the bedroom closet door and pulled the first shirt she could find off a hanger. It was Eddie's shirt and it hung loosely to her hips. She stepped out of the pajama bottoms and took a pair of old jeans from a hanger, huffing and puffing as she yanked them on.

She had never liked unannounced visitors, especially when she looked like this and was up to her neck in furniture polish and household chores. Remembering the smell of polish on herself, she went to the bathroom and squirted a dab of lotion onto her hands, softly rubbing the place where she removed the splinter. Then she went to the living room and waited for a knock at the front door.

It was quiet, no one came. She went to the door and opened it. No one was in sight. It was calm and serene outside. Jays flew up to the trees from the driveway when she opened the door.

"How strange," she said, and went back inside.

She returned to the bedroom and took some clean floral sheets and pillowcases off a shelf. She made the bed and was smoothing out the large white comforter on it when the voices started again. Again she went to the window, but there was still no one outside. She ignored the voices in annoyance, placed the rugs down on the floor, and then vacuumed each one. When she turned off the vacuum cleaner, the voices were near the window.

The female voice was elderly, the male voice was younger. They spoke in another language. She sat on the bed and listened. The female voice nearly whined as it described her condition. The male voice calmed the other one. It was full of compassion, patience, and gentleness. The language they spoke was vaguely familiar to Maxine.

After listening for a few minutes without the voices going away, she went to open the front door. No one was there. Maxine was very puzzled. The nearest house was over five hundred feet from hers. Who else would be here if not unexpected visitors? She went back inside and sat down near the front door. She waited to hear the voices and quickly spring open the door on them.

She waited over half an hour but didn't hear anyone. In the meantime, she brought order to the living room, dusting and shifting things around. She almost completely forgot about the voices as she moved to the bathroom to start cleaning there. Then, very clearly, she heard the female voice again. It was near tears.

Maxine's head peeked out of the bathroom slowly, leaning toward the tearful voice again. She tiptoed into the next room. Here the voices sounded as if they were just outside, but this room was near the back of the house. She did not understand why visitors would come to the back door instead of the front.

Expecting someone to knock, she dashed to the back door and waited. This door had a window draped by dark brown curtains. They were pulled together. The voices were silent, and now it seemed as if no one was on the other side. Maxine was very disturbed then because out of some forgotten place in her mind, she realized the language of the visitors was just on the tip of her tongue. She'd heard it a long time ago, far away from here. It sounded like the language her elders spoke, but she couldn't be sure.

When the voices began once more, she paused uncertainly. Her ability to understand what the voices said, either intuitively or with real knowledge of a forgotten tongue, was surprising. She stopped momentarily and seriously thought about it. How did she know it? How did she remember something she hadn't heard in so long?

The voices were close. The woman's voice was sad and wistful. The man's voice was still tender and gentle.

Maxine hesitantly lifted a finger and pulled back the curtain on the right side of the window just enough to peek through. Her eyes opened wide, glistening like abalone moons in the darkened porch area, and her mouth dropped open.

Right outside the door, at the bottom step, sat the two strange dogs she had seen earlier at the edge of the yard. The red one sat on the right side of the step; the brown one was on the left. They faced each other. They were not more than three feet away.

When Maxine moved the curtain, the dogs looked up and stared directly at her. An immeasurable amount of time passed between them in that instant. The red dog had black opal eyes, and the brown one's eyes were amber. After they saw Maxine, both of them stood, turned around and walked away from each other, in the opposite direction.

Maxine stood at the window for several minutes, unable to move. Then she went back into the living room and lay down on the couch. She spent the rest of the day in a daze.

When Eddie came home about five, he knew something was wrong. Maxine stared blankly at him and the skimpy meal she had prepared. Over the meal, she told him what she had seen that day and what she had heard.

He listened calmly and pushed the ringlets back from her face. When she said that she had to go home, hundreds of miles away, he agreed that she should.

*   *   *

Maxine and Eddie sat in the house with Maxine's old folks. It was late, after eleven, and one dim lamp lit the large room.

Maxine's grandfather sat across from her at the table and her grandmother sat to her right. They had pushed their teacups away, and these were at the center of the table along with a porcelain sugar bowl.

"Picked tea this afternoon," her grandmother said with a yawn, "from out by the fence. Bushes of it out there."

Maxine nodded politely and then turned the conversation to the purpose of their visit.

"Had an unusual thing happen to me not too long ago and wanted to ask you about it," she said.

Her grandfather raised an eyebrow at her and shut his mouth. Her grandmother nodded and waited.

Maxine watched their faces for a reaction to what she was going to say. "I don't want you old folks to think I'm crazy or anything like that, and I don't want to worry you none, but recently I heard a strange thing. Heard two dogs talking to each other. *Talking. They were talking Indian.*"

Her grandmother pursed her lips together and was thoughtful.

Maxine looked at her grandfather. He reached for a teacup and stared into it.

"Well?" Maxine asked when neither said anything.

Her grandfather shrugged and repeated, "Well?"

"But isn't that strange?" she asked. "Isn't something wrong with that?"

Her grandmother pushed her lips up in a straight tight line and shook her head no. Her grandfather mirrored this reaction.

"What did the dogs say?" he asked and folded his arms across his chest.

Maxine told her story. She ended by saying, "I don't know how I knew what they said, but I did. Isn't that strange?" she repeated.

"No, it's not strange," her grandmother said. "It's wonderful."

Maxine wasn't sure she heard correctly. She leaned toward her grandfather and asked, "Isn't there something wrong with hearing and seeing something unusual like that? Something wrong with *me,* or something wrong with *those dogs?*"

Her grandfather laughed. "Not the way we see things around here. May be that way for other people. We're not other people. What you saw and heard means that something is *right.*"

"I'm not going crazy?" Maxine asked in relief.

Her grandfather and grandmother shook their heads no. Her grandmother said, "Ain't been no crazy people in our family, in our tribe, until just recently." She was serious but it was Maxine's turn to laugh.

Her grandfather said, "All Indians know that animals talk, that ain't nothing new. But I hear tell that to see and hear talking animals today means lots of different things to different Indian people."

"Some tribes say its a bad sign of things to come. They say it foretells illness, bad events, and even bad medicine and thought used against someone. But around here, the folks don't think of it like that. We're like our relatives farther north."

"First thing to know is that not everyone in the world will ever hear what you heard, Maxine. Remember that.

"Round here, this kind of person is respected. That's the second thing to think about. Remember it.

"Then the next thing to know is that an incident like this usually changes us somehow, when we know this truth, that animals do talk. Think about that, too.

"Then, also know that you are not alone in what you saw. But don't go around acting better than the rest of your folks because of it. On the other hand, don't go around acting as if you don't know this truth either. In other words, be responsible for what you have seen and now know firsthand. Live it like it is the truth it is, but be humble about it.

"Finally, the last thing to know is that you have something wonderful to look forward to in your lifetime. You are destined to see more wondrous things as you go along in life. This is how this knowledge goes."

Maxine wasn't sure that she fully understood.

Her grandfather continued. "I'll tell you a story, Maxine, because it's night and this is the best time to tell things like this, but also because you are one of my own.

"I, too, have heard dogs talk, and therefore understand what you mean." He stopped and looked at his granddaughter.

"It happened when I was just a boy about eight or nine. Back then there were no cars and no roads like there are today. One day, I was walking home from a neighbor's house after I jumped off the wagon that carried the rest of the family. Well, you know how little boys are. Instead of going straight home, as I promised my mother, I took a detour. I went down to the creek and played around there.

"There was always stray dogs around these hills and valleys back then, it seemed. Sometimes they came in packs, but every now and then, I'd see a lone one straggling around, looking for food. I had a soft heart. Always shared my food with them whenever I could.

"That day I came up the path by the creek. It was dark down there because of the deep woods, but the trees and creek was real pretty. It was quiet except for the fish jumping and a couple of birds who called as I went by.

"There was a place on the path that always kind of made me stop and look around every time I was there, because it was so peaceful and pretty. That place always took my breath away. I stopped there and threw a couple of pebbles into the water. I heard the echo go all the way down the creek. Then, unexpectedly, I heard some people talking on the other side of those trees. The trees were pretty thick. There never was anyone around there, except our folks, so the voices came as a surprise. I was kind of curious to see who they were. I crossed the creek, jumping from stone to stone, and climbed over a beaver dam. Pretty quick, I was on the other side.

"The voices kept on, and I was able to get right up to them before I showed myself. But instead of finding people, I discovered a pack of dogs. They looked at me and went off in all directions. I stood there for a while thinking about this and then I went home.

"As soon as I got there, my mother wanted to know how come it took me so long.

"I told her about the dogs, and she gave me her full attention. The word got around about what I saw and soon I noticed that all my folks were keeping a close eye on me. Later, I learned that this was because the whole tribe thought they had an old-time holy person in the making. But it didn't turn out exactly like the old days. Though I saw a lot of similar things in my lifetime, I am not a holy man in the real old-time tradition. I am just your grandfather, a two-legged who's heard dogs talk and other wonderful remarkable things. Turned out that everyone in my family was this way, but not one of them ever thought of him or herself as a "holy person" in the real grand, old-time, tradition. That's a funny thing too, cause nowadays I hear tell that there's a lot of people, who ain't our folks and know less than this, calling themselves medicine people in the real old-time tradition.

"Now I sit here, sixty years later, telling you the exact same thing my old folks told me as a teenager. The only thing that's different is I'm talking in a foreign language, one forced on us, but nevertheless, I'm still talking Indian. It's ironical.

"Maxine, Eddie, to hear dogs talk ain't so strange. What is strange is what has happened to our folks in the last five centuries. We've been through a lot. Because of that, on the surface it looks like we must have changed a lot, too. But we're still not what others want us to be. Strange. For some, we ain't real enough anymore. For some, we're still too Indian. Some says we're not Indians at all, or First Americans, or Native Americans. Some say we are.

"All I can tell you for sure is that there are forces and beings in the universe who know who we really are. They'll approach us today in exactly the same way they have always done. That relationship ain't changed at all.

"This is for the rest of our lives, for as long as we live. This is what others don't understand and bargain for. They will tire of playing medicine people when they realize that this arrangement is for a lifetime, from sunrise to sunset, and dark to light, day in and day out, for as long as one lives. That's a long time.

"Don't be afraid of this, Maxine. Don't be afraid of who you are."

Part Two
World View

As a child I believed that the whole world was Indian, that human beings would break down into Paw- nees, Otoes, Poncas, Osages, Sioux, and other tribes with whom I was already familiar, and that the universe itself was composed entirely of tribal visions and precepts. My contact had been almost entirely with my family and other tribal people, so there was not yet any rea- son to believe that the world was *not* made up of these people, and everything I saw and did in the world was, of course, interpreted and experienced through them. Later, this illusion, if this is what it was, while not ever completely dissipated, was definitely disturbed and up- set, pushed out of my mind, by the continuous intrusion of foreign things into the tribal world I had envisioned.

Before my contact with the outside world, I held a view of the universe that was quite whole in and of itself, and was nurturing, in the sense of instilling in me an identity and a way to behave in the com- pany of other tribal people and in relationship to the universe.

To me this view of my world was similar to a three-dimensional picture or snapshot that reflected the physical terrain of my home and the people who made it home. I held this picture close to my heart and for a few years it was my most important possession. In this picture, I always saw the entire tribe moving in the background as in a motion picture, with other relatives and ancestors in the foreground—poised just so in contrast to the background activity. At the center stood my grandparents. Sometimes my image was in the picture, standing in the shadow of my grandparents, or sometimes at its border, like the shadow of a photographer stretched out across the ground.

Even when I did not see myself or identify where I was in the picture, I was always in it somehow. How I managed to walk into this picture in the first place is a question that always intrigued me. Had I fallen into it as if it was a big fish bowl that caught me and all my relatives seen in it? When and where, exactly, did I enter it?

What had I brought to it as a part of a new generation, and what part of myself had coalesced and solidified as a result of my inclusion in it? Where did tribal genealogy end and *I* begin?

But just as important, how was I extricated from it, as eventually happened? Then, how did I step back into it after I was suddenly expelled or dropped from it? Finally, when did I begin to separate myself from this picture and the people in it, who up until then made up my reality and universe? In short, apart from the tribal world, where did my individuality and space begin? What thoughts, experiences, and beliefs were my own?

I was first cognizant of my own space and thoughts when I was perhaps three or four. Even though I am able to recollect earlier images and words, they are fleeting and fragmented. Awareness of my own consciousness was different and more profound than anything I had previously experienced. My thoughts became neatly ordered, as if they were clothing hung up on a line to dry. I reasoned this way: First I see a shirt, it's white, it belongs to my father, and next is a towel, followed by another towel, and then a dress. . . . This is how my thoughts appeared and were connected to each other. I observed, I remembered, I reasoned, I speculated. It was such a shocking experience to wake up "conscious" one minute and realize that there was so much more to life than met the eye. It filled me with exhilaration, and some anxiety as well.

These new feelings and observations started with Grandpa. From that west window of the house, I lay on the bed in the afternoons and watched him go back and forth. One day, for some unknown reason, out of the blue it occurred to me that he might not be able to be there all the time. I accepted that. There were days when he *was* gone. Then I took one step further and imagined him absent for longer than a day. What if he was suddenly gone forever, whatever that meant? This thought sent waves of shock through me, not fear that it could conceivably happen, but that I *thought* it, all by myself, at the age I was, even with how little I knew about life, and despite knowing, instinctively, how defenseless I was against the harmful things in the universe in comparison to him. My tender age and unworldliness did not impede the thought at all.

This experience led me to notice Grandpa even more. I watched his dark hands as they worked, his posture and form as he walked away from me, and the ear flaps on his winter cap wrapped around his brown face. I became aware that things could change, *would* change by his prolonged absence.

He and I shared a very special relationship. I was his shadow, too. Wherever he went, I tried to follow along. Whether it was out into the fields on blistery hot days, or trips into town, or a walk or a ride to the mailbox, I fought to go. Sometimes it worked and I climbed up on one of the wagons our people were still driving into the mid-50s, and took my place beside him. As we rode along, he talked to me and the horses, and often he sang songs. Sometimes we traveled in silence with the horses' hooves the only sound beside the creaking of the wagon wheels and the splintery board we sat on. We studied the sunflowers, the shape and texture of leaves and other vegetation. The sky was far above us, yet we reached out and touched it, and the clouds seemed to move or stir in my hands and slip through my clumsy fingers.

He let the wagon roll slowly over the wooden bridges, the horses clip-clopping along, below us, glassy red water that was warm to the touch and rippled forever whenever I threw a pebble into it. Sometime a fish jumped, or one of the many species of birds in the forest of trees marking the creekbanks cried and flew down to us, settling for a moment on a floating log or at the water's edge. The horses waited on the bridge, snorting, and lifting a foot occasionally, stamping it, until we climbed on the wagon and Grandpa told them to take us home again. The rides were always the same, magic journeys that filled me with mystical energy for life.

When we walked, Grandpa and I moved at the same pace. Even now I am still able to see the tip of his cane touch the ground beside my foot. He pointed to objects, often not naming or discussing them. He pointed at them with his cane, then he stopped and studied them for a while from different angles, and then we moved on. This was the way I came into contact with things.

A lot of times I could not go with Grandpa, though. He was very firm about it. He'd shake his head no, look me sternly in my eyes, spit tobacco on the ground or in a can, and leave without me. Usually I'd cry, as children are prone to do. It was at these times that I seemed first able to get a sense of myself as capable of moving out of the picture. Until then, there was no separation. I felt as if I was the size of a teardrop, pulled into a gigantic whirlpool of deep, rapid water that swirled everything around, and from which I was inseparable.

Although Grandpa dominated my thoughts in this period, as soon as I realized that one day he might be gone, other new things I had never considered entered my mind. The first of these was the question, where would Grandpa *go* or *be* in his absence? It seemed to me, even then at that age, that he had to *be somewhere.*

I did not associate absence with death or finality. It was only absence, and temporary. I had seen death by then, though not of human beings whom I loved. But because we lived on a farm, I had seen animals die.

One cold winter day, my grandmother dressed me warmly and sent me outside to follow Grandpa around. The sun was shining, but the trees were coated with ice and their branches were thickly frozen. I broke off an icicle and walked around the barn, noting my tracks in the snow. I came upon some other tracks and decided to follow them. They led to three frozen yellow-striped cats stretched out in a patch where flowers grew in the summer, a mother and two kittens. The cats were stiff, and their fur had already lost its sheen and luster. I stood over them a long time, silently, the way I had studied the black tarantulas and snakes Grandpa had followed and pointed out with his cane, simultaneously aware of the deadness of the cats, the sun overhead, and my shadow settling and moving at my feet.

For several days afterward, watching Grandpa through the window, I thought about the frozen cats and how their bodies had been emptied of sound and movement; emptied of meows and soft, snarling hisses; and I thought of the weightlessness of their bodies as they jumped and ran across the ground. Now their bodies were heavy and stiff. Again, it seemed to me that those sounds and energy had to go somewhere.

Reflecting upon this stage of my development, I later wrote:

I was raised by my grandparents until I was school age. I was very observant, watching the world (environment) and people (grandparents) around me.

I began thinking about "life" when I was about five. The subject impressed me and hit me hard enough that I recollect to this day where I was in the house and what I was doing at the time.

I remember asking (in my head) what was life for, why did anyone (or anything) live, and why did I live. At that point death to me was a word that represented very little fear. I had seen things die, animals and such, and heard of people dying and saw evidence of it. I remember thinking that from what I could tell or see, there were only two things that were "real," and the wonder of both: life and death.

Comically, too, I also remember thinking that since I was "alive" (as far as I knew), I would try my best to "live" and if things didn't work out for me, then I would simply die. . . . The point is that I have been grasping at (comprehending) life and death, the unfathomable meaning of each since then. They still impress me as the only two things that are "real."[1]

My world did change, brought about by the death of my grandfather. Following this event I became more detached from the picture I had always associated myself with. I felt alone in the crowd of tribal people that still surrounded me.

His was the first death I experienced of anyone close to me. However, because the Otoe-Missouria view death in a way that is unique to themselves, death was never presented to us children as fearsome or evil. We did not fear the dead, either.

I tried to capture this particular view of death in my novel, *Ghost Singer,* in the words of the character Anna Snake.

> *If LeClair was around now, maybe she could talk to LeClair about this. But everyone said LeClair was dead, and Anna had seen him too at the funeral. He did look deader than a doornail then. She quickly touched her hand to her forehead regretting her last thought and looked ashamed. It was so disrespectful to LeClair. She sighed. It was just that she, now into her seventies, seemed to view life differently than at eighteen. For one thing, she was more convinced than ever now that people didn't die for nothing. There was a purpose to it, to being born, to living, and then to dying.*
>
> *She herself had seen people, following their deaths, on several occasions. But many of the Oklahoma tribal people found that to be a normal experience. From this Anna discovered that these people who had passed on didn't look any worse for going to the next world. On the contrary, they looked to be in one piece, whole and okay, as far as Anna could tell. Shoot, some looked better in death than they had in life, no pain, no suffering. Like Anna's people around her, she was taught to not be fearful, or ashamed, of these experiences of seeing deceased people. Actually, Anna*

smiled, according to her people's way of thinking, some-
thing would have been wrong with her if she didn't see be-
yond this world. It would mean that her senses didn't work,
and that she—in a way—was handicapped by her own lack
of sensitivity.

And on each occasion of seeing someone who had re-
cently passed away, Anna had learned a fraction more about
living and dying. . . . The continual appearance and pres-
ence of people who had gone on had consistently reaffirmed
for herself and other tribal people, that there was something
more to existence beyond death. The tribes knew it all along.
Even in the burial ceremonies, this was a prime consider-
ation in how the deceased was buried and treated. [2]

With Grandpa's burial, my world turned upside-down. I felt very
separated from what then began to happen. Of course, Grandma was
more affected. She found herself often alone with me and an empty
house. For a few years she carried on, staying there and even bringing her children back to plow the fields. She worked with them in the
hot sun. She was always strong, up to the very last. She had spunk and
could be a feisty old woman when it was required of her.

There were many facets to her that I found quite miraculous. She
was able to wrestle snakes from the trees and sweep them out of the
house, and work like a man baling hay in the barn. At times she was
more stubborn than a mule, summing up her feelings with one word,
saying "Humph!" through a closed mouth and pursed lips. Other times
she expressed sensitivity and tenderness like no other person I've ever
known.

In this period, Grandma told many a story. Though I was not supposed to listen to most of them, she had already introduced me to stories that dealt with infidelity, jealousy, sexual behavior, and so forth.
Because she told these stories so expressively and graphically, I
remembered not the entire stories as much as her *telling* the story. She
was it, *the story* of the story.

Sometimes I hid under the round kitchen table, listening to her speak to my aunts, waiting for one of her stories. She repeated gossip in the way of an omniscient narrator—not present, but able to describe the most minute detail of whatever had happened, those who were there, and all the words that were exchanged without interjecting her own comments or perspective. After this impersonal account was given, she filled in the background on what led up to this, and why things occurred as they did. Between the two accounts, she fleshed out the story and elaborated on everything. She was my first teacher in storytelling.

Her stories added something else to the tribal picture I held at the time: a three-dimensional quality that made certain things appear closer to me while other things receded into the background. They also added color, a mood or feeling that I experienced similarly, later in my life, only in painting. Besides setting up a storyteller framework, and thoroughly entertaining and immersing me in a story, she always left me wondering about it. I came to realize that to be enthralled this way by any story had as much to do with the storyteller as the story.

So I was her audience for a few years after Grandpa died. And in my picture of life at that age, my hand was always entwined with hers, or else I clung to her skirts so she would not leave me behind. Instinctively I knew that if our hands ever let go of one another, or if I let go of her skirts, I might slip off the picture and slide down into I-don't-know-where.

When I became school age, I was returned to my parents. This was an extremely traumatic experience because I had been mostly living with my grandparents since I was very young. This act, in itself, loosened my grip on the picture of a completely tribal world, and also my grip on Grandma. Afterward, I spent weekends and summers with her, but something had started to come between us, distance and separation caused by more than mere miles.

A chain reaction began when I was in the second grade that, once started, reverberated through my world. For the first time, the picture I was always able to envision began to dim. I seemed to float alone in space with nothing to pin me down, cut away from the safe and nurturing world that my grandparents had given to me.

First, my youngest sister developed tubercular meningitis at about the age of two. She had always been so smart, and now she began to hold her head and scream. She was quickly hospitalized and was eventually gone for four years. During that time she became completely paralyzed and had to relearn to walk and talk again.

Just as suddenly, it seemed, my mother was told that she had tuberculosis and she, too, was whisked away. I had one other sister, a year younger than I, and we found ourselves, with little warning, alone with our father. At first we were placed with our Pawnee grandmother, then our Otoe grandmother. Then my father, not sure that he could take care of us, work, and visit both my mother and sister in two different hospitals in two different towns, each several miles away, decided to put us in a government boarding school.

My Otoe grandmother took us over there and dropped us off. This was the first time my sister and I were completely separated from our family. I was seven or eight, in third grade, and my sister was in the first grade. The picture of the Otoe world was not yet entirely gone, but it was now *away* from me. I could *almost* see it, but I was definitely outside of it.

So my sister and I went to Pawnee boarding school. She had a harder time adjusting to the regimentation than I did, even though she had been looking forward to going to school. We survived the boarding school experience, and in reflection, it did offer one or two things not available to us at home. One of these was constant supervision. In my father's position, it was doubtful that he could have overseen us this closely. And we were "taken care of," in the sense that we were provided clothing, a place to sleep, and we had food in our mouths.

I actually recall very little of those two years. *Here* is where my lapses of memory begin. Perhaps, I now think, this was caused by feeling I had no control of what was happening to me.

After two years we went home. That period of time had been just long enough to sever a tie between all of us, at least from my point of view. The relationship between me and my Otoe grandmother was never the same again. And that with my parents was still fairly fragile. The picture I held of myself forever enmeshed with the Otoe world was now really gone.

From then on, my experience with school continued in this vein. It took me further and further away from the place I was born, though that place or world was just outside the school doors.

I attended public school from the fifth through the eleventh grades. There weren't many other Indian students, perhaps only a dozen besides myself, in one of the larger towns in Oklahoma where I lived with my mother and father.

Unfortunately, most of the things I learned at this time had nothing to do with a positive formal education experience. The instruction and values received in school, in fact, seemed to contradict earlier tribal teachings. With each higher grade, I felt a bit more out of sync with the tribal worlds I came from.

Books had something to do with this alienation. In the earliest school years, I was very drawn to books. They were so entertaining and informative, they opened up other worlds to me. When I learned to read, I was curious about what the books said about Indian people. Imagine how it felt to read the lies and distortions! Imagine how it felt to discover the omission of an entire race of people! Imagine my rage toward the adults who were in control of these things! The schooling process and books seemed to have a common goal: to deny the continuing existence of Indian people.

I literally turned against books and the educational system. I did not reveal my feelings and thoughts to anyone except my sister. Fearful of bothering Grandma with these angry thoughts, though it was still in her that I confided most often, everything remained bottled up inside.

A dramatic personal change occurred. I stopped believing in *everything*. I did not even remember that I once held a wondrous vision of my world, or that an ancient tribal voice would beckon if I listened. Where *did* I fit? No one could answer this question any better than I. School was enormously disorienting. The only answers were in the tribal voice I had helped plug my ears from hearing. Each day I turned further away from the people that I had loved. Fury for their human condition, and mine, consumed me. I tried not to go to school anymore, and my recklessness escalated. By the age of fifteen, I had experienced several major crises.

In this troubled time, my deceased grandfather called to me a couple of times. The picture I once tenderly held of the Otoe world began to return to me again, but it was not whole. Broken pieces of it drifted in and out of my mind. Much later I discovered great gaps of memory from that period as I tried to fit events together in a chronological sequence.

I realized that in order to survive and keep my sanity, I had to leave the place I was born. At the age of sixteen, in 1963, I left Oklahoma for a boarding school in New Mexico. Although I arrived in Sante Fe alone and lost, it was there that I was given new energy, new life. Santa Fe restored my spirit and my tribal identity. Living under the Sangre de Cristo mountains were Indian people who had no doubts about *their* identity or *mine*. This interaction was very healing. Hundreds of miles from Oklahoma, I had come home.

About a year later in Santa Fe, I timidly began to write. Words poured out, page after page. I am still amazed by it, by the torrent of thoughts deposited there. Many things prompted my writing, but most of all it grew out of a wonderful school that I attended, the environment of the Institute of American Indian Arts (IAIA), an art school that rose to national prominence in the years that followed. IAIA was totally unlike any school I had ever experienced.

Although I took a writing class there, that wasn't why I went to the school. I wanted to learn how to paint. I studied under Charles Loloma first, and later, Fritz Scholder. My paintings weren't very promising though. Through these new activities, however, my picture of the Otoe world gradually came together. Santa Fe had everything to do with its restoration.

My writing during this period reflected the perilous route I had come. Much of it was not very good, but I could hear my own voice now, distinguish it from others. Writing released years of oppression. It made me whole and free. One piece in particular seemed to express my renewed self, the sense of identity that was given back to me when I stopped trying to follow the mainstream, stopped denying the tribal

essence of me, as I started listening for the familiar voice of tribal oral
tradition again.

> *My name is "I am living."*
> *My home is all directions and is everlasting.*
> *Instructed and carried to you by the wind,*
> *I have felt the feathers in pale clouds*
> *and bowed before the Sun*
> *who watches me from a blanket of faded blue.*
> *In a gentle whirlwind, I was shaken,*
> *made to see one earth in many ways,*
> *and when in awe my mouth fell open,*
> *I tasted a fine red clay.*
> *Its flavor has remained after uncounted days.*
> *This gave me cause to drink*
> *from a crystal stream*
> *that only I have seen.*
> *So I listened to all its flowing wisdom*
> *and learned from it a song.*
> *This song the wind and I*
> *have since sung together.*
> *Unknowingly, I was encircled*
> *by its water and cleansed.*
> *Naked and damp I was embraced and dried*
> *by the warmth of your presence.*
> *Dressed forever in the scent of dry cedar,*
> *I am purified and free.*
> *And I will not allow you to ignore me.*
> *I have brought to you a gift.*
> *It is all I have but it is yours.*
> *You may reach out and enfold it.*
> *It is only the strength in the caress*
> *of a gentle breeze. . .*
> *but it will carry you*
> *to meet the eagle in the sky.*

My name is "I am living." I am here.
My name is "I am living." I am here.

Notes:

1. Anna Lee Walters. *The Sacred: Ways of Knowledge, Sources of Life.* (Tsaile, Arizona: Navajo Community College Press, 1977), p. 329.

2. Anna Lee Walters. *Ghost Singer* (Flagstaff, Arizona: Northland Press, 1988), p. 125.

Buffalo Wallow Woman

My name is Buffalo Wallow Woman. This is my real name. I live on the sixth floor of the whiteman hospital, in the mental ward. This is not the first time I have been in a mental ward, I know these places well. I wander through this one like a ghost in my wrinkled gown. My feet barely brush over the white tile floor. The long windows reflect the ghost that I have become: I am all bones and long coarse white hair. Nevertheless, there are slender black iron bars on the windows to prevent my shadow from leaving here. Bars on sixth-story windows puzzle me. On the other side of the bars, the city lays safely beyond my reach, the wrath of the ghost of Buffalo Wallow Woman.

Bars or not, I plan to leave this ward tonight. I've already been here too long. This place makes me ill, makes my heart pause and flutter. Sometimes it makes me really crazy. I told that to those in white, but they refused to listen, with the exception of one. I said, "Hospitals make me sick! Here my strong heart is weak." In response, one of them shrugged, another frowned suspiciously. A nurse replied, "Now, Mrs. Smith, you don't want to hurt our feelings, do you?"

Well, that made me grab her arm and dig my long fingernails into it. I wanted to scream but I controlled this urge and said calmly, "What's that you called me? My name is Buffalo Wallow Woman." She and I stared each other in the eyes for five minutes before we separated: she to her mindless patients, and me to my room to locate the clothes I ought to wear when I escape from here.

My clothes are missing. Why would someone take a ghost's clothing? My possessions are so old. My moccasin soles consist only of patches by now, but I don't care. They take me where I want to go. I look at my feet stuffed into polyfoam and I hunger for beautiful things that are no more.

The closet is empty. Perhaps my clothes were never there. Perhaps I really am a ghost now. Perhaps I did not live at all. I look in the window to reassure myself—my spirit shimmers and fades, shimmers and fades. Am I deceased or alive? At this moment I really don't know.

I float down the hall, going from room to room. I search each one. Because I am a ghost, I go where I please. No one takes me seriously. Those who see me stare for a minute and decide to ignore the bag of bones and wild white hair that I have become. They underestimate me. They do not believe that I am really here. Down the hall and back again I haunt the ward. My clothes are not anywhere on this floor. I return to my room, climb upon the bed like a large clumsy child. I am waiting for nightfall, hours away, to make my departure. After all I've been through, this brief wait is nothing to Buffalo Wallow Woman.

Through the barred window, clouds fly rapidly to the north. They call to me. By name they know me. *Buffalo Wallow Woman,* they whisper through the glass and the bars to remind me who the old bag of bones is and why I am here. I lift my head and square my sagging shoulders.

Far away, I hear a melody flow toward me. It is from my people's golden age and it has found me in this insane place where I am now held without respect or honor. A thousand years ago, or yesterday, in the seasons of my youth, my people danced and sang to the cloud beings in spectacular ceremony as the cloud beings gathered to shoot arrows of zigzag lightning and fiery thunderbolts across the sky. The cloud beings darkened to spirals of purple and dark red. They all twisted and turned in space like the mighty and powerful beings they truly were. And in the torrents of rain to fall later, slapping down upon the earth, filling the dry beds there to overflowing, my people lifted their heads and drank the rain thirstily. Afterward, with that taste still in their mouths, they sang in unison, "O you! That mystery in the sky!"

Miraculously, the words return to me in this alien room. I feel the wind of those clouds blow across my face, the raindrops splash the crown of my head one at a time. My face and hair feels soaked with rain. I lift my face and open my mouth. I sing, "*Hey yah hah O!*"

My voice is as small as a red ant. It is swept away in the noises coming from the vents, crushed under the hospital sounds of announcements and rolling carts and beds going back and forth in the hallway. My room is suddenly quiet and dry. The clouds are disappearing in the sky, too. Bah! There is no magic in man-made places like this. This is why Buffalo Wallow Woman always brings it with her.

I look at my wrinkled hands. They are wide and large-boned. My nails are faded yellow and longer than they need to be. I wish I could hold a birchbark rattle with painted streaks of blue lightning on it in my idle fingers. I would shake it this way and that, in the manner of my people. They lifted their rattles to the cloud beings and shook them softly in that direction. To show the departing cloud beings that I remember who they are, their magnificent splendor and power, and also who I am, I stand on the step to my bed and face them. I lift the imaginary rattle and shake it just so. A soft hiss emanates from it.

Behind me, someone says, "Mrs. Smith."

I see part of him in the window. He is the doctor who arrives each day to study me, but now I am tired of him and I think he is tired of me as well. Nothing has been exchanged between us, and he always arrives at times like this. I look at the bars before I look at him.

I think of the animals my men have taken in communal hunts before there were grocery and convenience stores. The beautiful glassy eyes of a dozen soft-brown deer people stare at me from the walls of this room. They look me right in the eye, but I do not flinch. They say, *Buffalo Wallow Woman, here we are.* I see the trail of their last misty breaths arch up into the sky—rainbows they are. I hear a shaggy buffalo bull as he turns his great frame to face me. I see the dust rise in smoky spirals under his trotting hooves as he charges toward me. His breath is hot steam on my face.

Then come the human sounds, the footsteps, a pumping heart, blood rushing to the face, and the promised words of appeasement to the animals as they silently fall with a shattering thud, offering themselves to us. For this ultimate gift, we offered everything in return, our very lives were traded on the spot, and those animal people taught us thousands of prayers and songs to honor their spirits and souls from then on. In that way they permitted us to live, and they too lived with us. That is how we mutually survived all those years. The man behind me, the man who is here to help, doesn't know this.

He occupies the chair near the door.

"Do you come with prayers?" I ask. I turn to face him. The eyes of the deer and buffalo people surround us. They wait for his answer.

He is tall and angular with dark hair standing straight up. His eyes are foreign to me, colorless and jumpy, as if they must run somewhere. He glances behind him, over his shoulder. I am the one suspended here, but he acts trapped too. "If you come with prayers, I'll talk to you," I say, trying to figure out this odd creature whose habitat I do not know. Each day his behavior and appearance has become more unsettled. His presence disturbs the room.

He decides to speak. His voice booms at me. "Mrs. Smith, do you know how long you've been here? Do you understand that you have made no progress at all?" He is angry at me for being here.

I refuse to answer for this. I zip my lips together but I face him head-on. I have time, lots of time. I can outwait him. I become the ghost again. I start to disintegrate before him.

"Now don't do that!" he orders. He rubs his eyes and runs a hand through his wiry hair. His eyes dart everywhere. His breathing is rapid. He manages to hold his eyes in one place for a few seconds and he forcibly calms himself. He moves closer to me.

"All right, Buffalo Wallow Woman, if that's who you say you are, how did you get here? Do you know where you are?" He is still brusque and impatient, but he has called me by my real name and I must reply. My body becomes more solid and earthly again. I lean toward him.

"Do you come with prayers?" I venture again in my small voice.

"What kind of prayers?" he asks.

"Prayers to the spirits of those whose fate is in your hands." My voice is like the red ant again, crawling quietly across the room.

"What do you mean? I don't understand," he says while his eyes jump all over.

"You have no prayers then?" I persist.

"No!" he says.

"It is as I feared," I answer, turning away from him. "That is why I must leave here. Ghosts and spirits long for them. The hearts of human beings cannot beat steadily without them for long either. I know my own can't." I stand on the stepstool to move down to the floor.

"You aren't going anywhere. You don't know where you are, let alone who you are!"

We are almost the same height now. I stand before him, and he observes me from his throne.

"Where are my clothes?" I ask in my most rational voice. "I am going to leave here tonight."

He ignores me.

"You're very ill," he says with a frown. "You have no family, no one to take care of you. With your bad heart, you may not last long outside of here."

This time there is something in his voice I haven't heard before, but I want him to go. I seal my lips, and he sees immediately what I have done. He stands and goes. The room settles again.

* * *

For several weeks, there has been one in white here who is unlike this doctor and the others. Today she will appear when the sun reaches the third bar in the window. It will be soon now. In the meantime, I decide to haunt the hallway once more. I've covered its distance at least a dozen times each day for the last three months. It is the only exercise the patients have. I think of wolves in zoos, running in circles inside their cages, as I leave my room.

Today I look carefully at the occupants of each room and those people in the hallway. There are thin walls separating the two, skinny lines that distinguish the patients from the staff. I can't tell them apart except by their clothing. If truth be known, the doctors and staff may be more quirky than the others. We patients just show our quirkiness.

In Room 612 sits a skeleton with frozen eyes. I am drawn to it, magnetized by its forceful pull. "I am a ghost," I confess to it. The skeleton does not move at all. Something whispers to me that its spirit is gone. I look around the room for it but I am the only ghost here. I leave 612 and go across the hall.

The man there is waiting for me. He embraces me tenderly and strokes my wild white hair. He calls me Grandmama and weeps on my gown. I sit down beside him, we stare into each other's souls while he holds my hand. He babbles at me, I nod. He weeps until his eyes are bright red. Then, exhausted, he lays down on his high bed. Asleep, he relaxes his grip on me and I move on.

Two nights ago, a hysterical young woman was brought into the next room. There she sits now, sullen and old before her time. Her wrists are wrapped in white bandages. I pause at the door. She raises a hand and a finger at me. "I am a ghost," I say. "That means nothing to me."

My words anger her. She rises abruptly to rush at me but hesitates after a step or two to clutch her belly and groan. It is then I notice the rise of it under her gown. I go to her rescue and she leans on me, breathing hard. Her eyes are scared.

"You would kill your child?" I ask as she bends into me. The moment passes, and she is able to stand on her own.

"Not my child," she said, "me!" Then she looks at me and adds, "I thought you were a ghost."

"I am," I repeat. This is our introduction to one another.

There is a loud disturbance in the hall, scuffling and a shouting exchange of words. One of the hospital staff is wrestling a middle-aged man. I and the young woman go to the door to watch. All the way down the hall, different colored faces appear in the doorways of each room like wooden masks. The faces are expressionless and blank, like those on the street.

The patient is overpowered and wrestled to the floor before our eyes. A silver needle punctures his arm. After the initial outburst of anger, the whole scene takes place in silence. The patient is lifted up, whisked away. The staff quickly tidies the area as if nothing happened and the hall clears. Seconds later, no one remembers what just occurred.

Only the young woman and I remain. She asks if the incident really took place. I say, "That's what will happen to all of us if we don't do what they say." The girl frowns at the bars on the windows. She has just discovered them.

"When you leave here, you must live," I say. "If you don't see to your child, it could end up here."

The girl is confused. She looks at her bandaged wrists and again at the bars. She rubs her belly. I leave her there, alone and troubled. I make my way down the hall, looking in on each person in each room along the way.

Most everyone, patients and staff alike, look right through me. My presence is not acknowledged at all. Quite unexpectedly, from deep within me, I feel the wrath of Buffalo Wallow Woman for this indignity. My blood begins to boil. It is hot and dangerously close to making me explode! My heart flaps against my chest, voices caution me.

I pause and reflect on this feeling. That old fire still burns? Rage, this overpowering, is still a part of Buffalo Wallow Woman? How very strange. I thought that I had given up this human feeling years ago, the very first time I went into a mental hospital. I mutter my thoughts aloud and head toward my room.

Back there, Tina awaits. She is nervous, frantic, because of what I am about to do. Her soft voice is usually a coo. Now it is high and squeaky.

"Where were you?" she asks tensely. "For a minute I thought maybe you had already gone." She rushes toward me and embraces me.

I pat her tiny hand. "It's not time yet." I go to my bed, climb upon it, and say, "My clothes are gone, but where I am going, clothes don't matter I guess."

The first day Tina walked into my room I knew who she was. It was evident in her dark hair and high cheekbones, though her skin was more fair than mine. But where it really showed was in her behavior and her usually carefully chosen words. She was such a tiny thing. She carried bed pans past my door all day before she finally came in.

She read my name on the door and over the bed. "Mrs. Smith," she said, "I'm Tina. I'll be your evening nurse until you leave here, or until the shifts change in a few weeks, whichever comes first."

I stood at the door and watched her adjust my bed.

"It's Buffalo Wallow Woman, Tina, not Mrs. Smith," I responded, "and I am a ghost."

"I know," she replied seriously, "I've heard."

She gave me a red lollipop from a pocket and asked, "Why are you here Buffalo Wallow Woman, if you don't mind me being so direct?"

I tore the shiny wrapper off the lollipop and stuck it in my mouth. I didn't answer. I sucked on the candy and counted the bars on the window, the way I did with the doctor when I wanted him to leave.

"Why are you here Buffalo Wallow Woman?" she asked again.

I sucked the candy hard and motioned that my lips were sealed. I climbed on the bed, sure that she would leave.

Instead, she pulled out a wire hairbrush from the nightstand and answered with a mischievous smile, "If I ask you four times, and if you really are Buffalo Wallow Woman, then you will have to tell me, won't you?"

She began to comb my hair, pulling my head here and there. "Ghost hair is hard to comb," I said, as if this was our secret.

She replied, "You are not a ghost, Buffalo Wallow Woman. Do ghosts like lollipops?"

"Ghosts like a lot of earthly things," I said. "That's what often keeps us here."

"Why are you here Buffalo Wallow Woman?" she asked a third

time, and I knew then that I wanted someone like her, someone important, to know.

She braided my hair tightly around my head. Her fingers flew.

"I'm lost, Tina," I said. "I'm caught between two worlds, a living one and a dead one. This is the dead one," I motioned out in the hall, "right here. And this is the root of my illness. I have to return to the living one in order to be whole and well."

Tina's fingers stopped a second. She chuckled, "This is the dead one? How do you figure that?"

"Look around," I answered. "There is no magic here because everything is dead. I think that only ghosts are capable of surviving here."

Before I realized it, she asked me the fourth time. "Why are you here Buffalo Wallow Woman?" She pulled a chair close to me as if she really planned to listen.

I decided to tell. I composed my thoughts for a moment and then began. "I am the ghost of Buffalo Wallow Woman. Do you know what a Buffalo Wallow is, my child?"

Tina nodded. "A watering hole, or something like that?" She reached over and held my hand as I spoke. Her hand was half the size of mine.

I asked, "Do you want to know about my name?" She nodded again.

"The name was taken about a hundred winters ago most recently, but I suppose it is older than that. It came out of a time when the animal people still had possession of the world. Then, they were the keepers of all sacred things.

"Wallows are shallow depressions in the earth that were made by most animals when they rolled around there and lay down. Several large ones are still visible today. They usually surround water holes or later become them because of the shallow bowls they eventually form. Today most of them, of course, are gone. They have either blown away, or towns or other things sit on top of them.

"The marshy areas that the wallows were, or became, often dried up as the summer days grew hot and long. Each, in turn, disappeared.

Some time ago, there was one large wallow with water, a buffalo wallow, left. All the others had turned to dust. It was a precious thing to all life then, especially to a stranded or lost human being. One day, there appeared on the horizon of that sacred place, a lost woman, on foot and traveling alone. The buffalo people stood up one by one when they saw her approach. They saw her stumble and fall from either weakness or illness, and the searing heat of the sun. Near the wallow, she collapsed and failed to rise again. One of the old buffalo bulls told two younger ones to go to her aid. The young bulls trotted through the evaporating marsh to the ailing woman. Behind them, where their hooves sunk into the marsh, pools of water began to gurgle and bubble up. They trotted around the stranger in circles until she lay in a dirty pool of water, but she was cooled and revived. Afterward, she received more help from the buffalo people and then was able to travel on. She took the name Buffalo Wallow Woman out of humility to the buffalo people, out of gratitude for her life. She understood that it was the buffalo people and the spirit of the wallow who gave her humility and gratitude, as well as her life. These were the lessons she had learned in the hands of the buffalo people."

Tina expected more. I promised, "Tomorrow I'll finish if you still want to know."

The next day she arrived in the afternoon and brought with her a dark green leaf of Indian tobacco and a small red tin ashtray. She lit the tobacco and burned it in the tray. The odor of that one small curled leaf filled the mental ward, but it was not enough to take away all the pain and fears contained on this floor. She hid the tray in the drawer just before another nurse popped in the room to ask what was burning.

Tina shrugged her shoulders and winked at me. "Would you mind if I called you something other than Mrs. Smith or Buffalo Wallow Woman? Where I come from we don't call each other by such names. One seems too formal and the other too sacred. Would I offend you if I called you Grandmother?" she asked politely.

I gazed at her with admiration and answered, "That would not offend me, my child. That would honor me. And if this is your plan and decision, then I must call you grandchild, if that's the way it is to be."

Tina offered her hand to me and I took it. This is the way we joined forces. When her schedule permitted, I resumed my story.

"Buffalo Wallow Woman died in the year of the great smallpox epidemic, near the very place she had been saved as a younger woman. This time, she and others who were sick isolated themselves from the remainder of the people and, therefore, did not receive formal burials.

"As a young girl of perhaps eleven or twelve winters, I visited this place unexpectedly. At the time I didn't know who Buffalo Wallow Woman was or her story. I had been traveling by wagon with my family through an unfamiliar stretch of open plains country that was partly frozen but was beginning to thaw in a sudden burst of sunshine. When the wagon became bogged down in deep gray clay, the men got off to dig out the back wheels. I, too, climbed off and noticed a place to the side of the wagon trail that tugged at me. It was a very large shallow pool covered with ice. Its size was perhaps half a city block. Birds were soaring overhead and chirping at me. I watched them dip toward the frozen pool and fly away in flocks. Soon my family had dug out the wagon and were ready to leave. By evening we had reached our destination, and I thought that I had already put the shallow pool out of my mind.

"But that night I dreamed of it. I saw it in all the four seasons. There were buffalo at the pool's edges, and their reflections were in the water with the clouds and sky. Other animals were also there, such as bears, deer, and all species of birds.

"Every night I dreamed of the pool, and it seemed to be speaking to me. Then one night, Buffalo Wallow Woman visited me in my dreams and in a mysterious way told me who she was and what had happened there. She said that she had not died after all, and that in another world she had learned that she never would. She said this was all true and because it was, our people had never lied to us. They understood everything all along.

"She told me that it was an old spirit who had called me to the watering hole, the same spirit that guided her there each time she was close to death, and for this reason, she and I were tied together by it. The same spirit had called the buffalo people, the bird people, and all the others who came to drink, because that spirit made no distinction between the life of a buffalo, a cloud, a mountain, a stone, or a human being. It was the same indescribable force, no matter what form it took.

"At my tender age, it was truly remarkable that I actually understood what Buffalo Wallow Woman said. It was wonderful that I understood she had claimed some invisible part of me, and I claimed some part of her, and I accepted our relationship without question. I could not understand with my head, though. I grasped it at the level of and at the center of my heart. I understood that I had been thirsty but didn't know it myself, and I had gone to the wallow so that my soul might drink. The spirit of the wallow knew me better than I knew myself."

Tina didn't press for more right then. She was quiet, staring outside at the evening sky. The room was quiet. We didn't speak about me again for several days. Then she came into the room and sat down without a word. She waited for me to continue.

"All my life, I have been told by the whiteman that I am crazy, my child," I picked up where I left off, "because I see things that other people do not. I hear voices that no one else does. But the craziest thing I do, they tell me, is take these visions and voices seriously. This is the way of all Buffalo Wallow Women, I suppose. I structure my life around the visions and voices because it pleases me to honor them this way. I am never alone because of this. It is my inheritance from Buffalo Wallow Woman, from my own flesh and blood, from the visions I have received, and from my identity as this kind of person.

"But each day the doctor asks me if I know who I am, and I have to bear this outrage. He also asks me if I know where I am. He talks about 'reality.' He tells me to face it, that this is, after all, a new time which has no room for Buffalo Wallow Women. His questions, pretensions, and arrogance are ludicrous to me. I feel that he is more ill than I am. I am Buffalo Wallow Woman! Wherever I go, the spirits go with me.

"I am suspect and feared because I admit that I am a ghost. This is dangerous, I am told. It is the one thing the doctors have said that I know to be true. I *am* dangerous. I am dangerous because my craziness may spread from me to another and on and on. I am dangerous because I still have some rage left about what's happened to me over the years. It's not entirely squelched yet, although I've tried to empty it out of me. This surprises even me at the moment. And I am dangerous because I have great destructive powers within me that I haven't used yet.

"For instance, I can kill with my eyes if I so desire. I can shoot out poison and make my victims squirm with agony. There's all kinds of poison for this, but most come from pure hate. I can use words in incantations that will steal the soul, the spirit, the will, and mind away."

Tina looked at me mischievously. Before she could speak, I said, "Now don't say a word until you walk through this ward, look closely at every patient, and are able to explain how they became that way!"

We ended here, and Tina left. That night, laying in the dark, I decided to ask Tina to help me escape this unbearable indignity of forced confinement. A few days passed before I voiced my question.

I said, "Tina, my child, I am going to escape from here, I am going to fly away. When the time comes, I would like you to be there, to help me at the very last."

Tina replied, "If you're a ghost, why can't you just go?

"It's not that easy. Some earthly person has to release me, you see."

She stood at the window staring at the iron bars. She turned around and asked, "You can really do it?"

I nodded.

She took a deep breath and crossed her heart like a small child. "O.K.," was all she said.

* * *

Now that the time is here, Tina seems reluctant to have me leave. She's had weeks to prepare, but her eyes are actually moist and red.

"Tell me I am doing the right thing," she says. "I mean, you're my patient, what am I doing?"

She is panicky. She flutters all around.

"You and I, my child, are more than patient and nurse, much more than that. Don't make our kinship so small, so insignificant. This is the stuff that links the whole chain of life together, old to young, grandchild to grandmother, and on and on."

It is dark outside. Not even the bars on the window can be seen. I climb off the bed. My nightgown floats loosely around me.

Tina is watching me. She has a large brown sack with her. When she speaks, her voice is calm. "I brought everything you asked of me, and something that I thought of myself." She takes out a thin red flannel blanket from her package, folds it in half, and puts it at the foot of the bed. "This is for you," she says.

"Thank you, my child," I answer, touched by her thoughtfulness. I pick up the blanket and hold it to my heart.

"What do you want me to do?" she asks. I see her hesitate before she moves.

I lift the blanket and ask her to lay it on the floor.

"Sit here." I point to one end of the blanket. She takes her sack with her. I sit down at the other end.

"Now," I say, "I want to speak to you before I leave. Please, child, put those things between us."

Tina lays out a pouch of green tobacco and cigarette papers, and the red ashtray. She puts a beaded butane lighter inside the tray.

I ask her to turn out the fluorescent lights over us. Only a soft light comes from the bathroom. The door to it is half closed. Then I ask her to take my hair down and pull off my shoes.

We sit together in silence for a long time, gathering our thoughts together for the last thing we are about to do for one another.

Finally, I am ready. I say, "My child, you are the answer to a prayer, the prayer of Buffalo Wallow Woman. To find you in a place like this is very sweet to someone like me. I feel a stab of victory for Buffalo Wallow Woman, for though she is a ghost, you are alive and are as strong and thoughtful as she has ever been.

"You came to me with open arms and received a ghost in them, and you did not flinch at anything I said. All of it you took in, in your strong, gentle way. You have been taught well. I have told you everything—good things, ugly things, sacred things, and unholy things. We have even sung together. You have given me honor and respect in a way that only kin can pay. In exchange for that, kin to kin, grandmother to grandchild, I want to include you in my prayer tonight.

"Everything I have told you these last few weeks is the truth, you know. Sometimes we ghosts are full of rage and anger, such as I have been at certain times, but the ghost of Buffalo Wallow Woman can only speak the truth, even when it hurts, as it sometimes does.

"Anyway, I thank you, child, for the honor you have brought me, by listening to me, by singing with me, by calling me your grandmother, by praying for me tonight, and by setting me free.

"I have spent a lifetime in and out of this insane place that the doctors call reality, or the real world. I have spent a lifetime waiting to be set free, because no one else but you could do it for me. This is what we mean to each other. This is what life means.

"These are my parting words to you, my child. Do you wish to say anything?"

Tina nods her head. I can almost hear the movements. The spirit people have come into the room. They surround us.

"You don't understand," she says. "I'm not what you want me to be. I have flaws. I went to school. I can't speak my language because of this. I don't want to live in poverty the way my family does. I'm weak, and worst of all, I'm not very spiritual."

She pauses, threatening to break into tears.

"And I agreed to this because I thought you would change your mind. I didn't think you would really go through with it. I never thought I would actually be here right now."

"But you are here," I answer. "You are here with the ghost of Buffalo Wallow Woman. Most of us never know what we will do at a certain moment until that moment arrives. Then we know. Do you have doubts now?"

"Not doubts," she says, "but lots of sadness."

"This is not a bad thing, Tina," I say. "Soon you will feel like singing out, *Hey yah hah O!*" I say. "I promise you that you will feel it in you."

I pick up a cigarette paper and the Indian tobacco and began to roll a smoke. I give it to Tina. I say, "When I have gone, you must light the smoke, then blow a puff to the earth and sky and then to the four directions. Then you must say in a clear voice, 'I offer this smoke for the spirit of my grandmother, Buffalo Wallow Woman. May she be forever at peace and may she forever live in nature all around me.' You must say this, Tina, not only think it."

The spirit people make noises all around me. Some of them are in the darkness, others are in the light.

Tina is flustered, but she acknowledges my directions.

I close my eyes and begin my prayer. "O Mystery of Life! The time has come for Buffalo Wallow Woman to depart," I say to the spirits in the room, the spirits that follow me everywhere. They agree with my words. Their voices answer *Yes* in chorus. I continue. "I want to leave this world without anger or hate, for in this final moment, I want none of that to remain. I leave this world to my grandchild sitting here. May she love it and care for it as much as her elders did. My final requests are that you spirits accept me and take me home, and that in my departure, you watch over my grandchild here."

My heart flaps against my breastbone. I feel it pause, flutter, and thump my breastbone again. I open my eyes. The room is cold. The spirits are everywhere. There are deer people, buffalo people, and cloud beings—so much life in one little room! They chant and sing.

I am strangely weightless and transparent. I feel myself break up into a fine, wet mist. Then, I am looking down from the ceiling. Tina sits alone. I see my body lying across the floor, a bag of old bones and long wild white hair.

Tina is holding the smoke. Her hand shakes violently. She looks up at the ceiling, takes a deep breath, and steadies herself. She picks up the beaded butane lighter and lights the sacred smoke. She tries to speak. Her words are timid and frightened. She clears her throat and starts again.

She says it all perfectly, word for word. The spirits answer joyfully, *Yes! Yes!* They turn to me and say, *Buffalo Wallow Woman, now you are free. No bars shall ever hold you again.*

The spirits guide me to the window, but now it is my turn to hesitate. I look back at Tina, my grandchild. She is sitting there all alone. She looks troubled and sad.

We'll always be here, the spirits say, and I nod. Then, as we begin to slip through the bars, I hear little Tina sing, *"Hey yah hah O!"*

Part Three
History

As an American Indian, I have been deeply disturbed by much of the literature pertaining to tribal people in the Americas. Furthermore, American history and its treatment of indigenous people is generally offensive and culturally biased. When indigenous people are included at all, the presumption is often negative and uninformed. But this popular literature has been widespread in mainstream society since the time of contact. Indeed, it is still in use in our educational systems today.

Eventually I saw the literary treatment of tribal peoples by nontribal writers as a way of maintaining the status quo of mainstream society. And the absence of individual Native voices interpreting their own identities and histories, appeared as a form of censure, as a form of suppression that was deeply rooted in American society. I began to evaluate tribal histories versus American history, and to study what history means to tribal societies, as compared to what history is to American (mainstream) society. How do tribal histories vary from American history in their perspectives, structure, and content? And how do tribal people relate to their own respective histories?

Perception of my own connection to both of my tribal histories and prehistories was through *family* lineage. Through lineage of clan, band, and family, I learned that tribal history was animate and alive, vested in individual or group tribal members whose responsibility it is to sustain this living quality in the oral descriptions of our existence and experience. This is what my grandfather and grandmother did through their religious activities and through their words: they kept history alive.

History in this context of family and lineage did not begin with human existence alone, however, because the Otoes, for example, were extensions of other life preceding human existence. Thus, five hundred years is a very brief time in the sweep of tribal histories. History also intermingles with art, religious activities, and philosophy, so that in tribal societies each area has implications for the others. The tribal historian is often knowledgeable in more than history because it corresponds and links to something else. One does not specialize solely in history, therefore, because to do so is to work and live in isolation from the community and universe.

Responsibility for recording and maintaining history in the tribes was and still is *shared*. Here there is often some distinction between male and female roles, depending upon the tribal group. In formal ceremonial life, history is passed from male to male, or female to female, as is prescribed in a particular ceremony, or by a clan, band, or family. In this way, each gender, clan, band, or family holds a vital part of tribal history that is recognized and acknowledged in formal gatherings and events.

History is contained in all tribal material culture (including medicine bundles), and ritual, ceremonies, formal storytelling, prayers, and songs. Because much of this culture is intangible, historians in the tribes are greatly valued and respected. And although it would appear that almost everyone would then be considered an historian to a certain extent under this arrangement, this is not so. Often families, clans, or bands have only one or two persons who are really knowledgeable about that group in a particular time frame. Nevertheless, all these pieces come together for periodic review and discussion, and in this way, facts and other information are consistently substantiated and verified.

In this exploration, I discovered two principle sequences of tribal history. The first starts at the beginning and works its way toward the present. The second starts with the present and works its way back to the beginning. Although there may be discussions on the history of the people moving to a particular place, for example—isolated events—often these historical notes seem to be just that until they are pinned down in this larger framework.

> *Let me tell you a story. This story is of my grandfather, on my mother's side. This happened while he was in Nebraska, before they were on the reservation.*
>
> *He went out hunting. He went off by himself. In those days when a man went hunting, he went early in the morning, by the break of day, and was back by noon or before. He went and he didn't have any luck. On his way back, he was tired. He lay down to rest and went to sleep. While he was laying there, he heard a sound. I guess you've heard birds that sound like an airplane. When it comes down it makes a whizzing sound. A bird came from above. After a while, the whizzing sound stopped. He heard a voice. It talked in a song. It said, "Come on, get up." It was a spirit that came and told him to come and get up. Well, he did that. And there was this figure of an Indian. It wasn't standing on the ground. It was up in the air. He looked at this figure. The next song said, "Come, and follow me." So the man followed. They went to a place where the figure sang another time, "Here it is." Then another figure appeared. This man seemed to be on top of a mountain, or a high ridge with a valley below where the village was. The second figure told the man, "Now watch, we are going to give you a talent. That is why we picked you out, so you can be useful to your people. Now watch, pay attention. Look at that village down there." The man watched.*

In the village there was commotion. Crying. Wailing. The people there were in a sad situation. The figures told the man, "Now you hear that? An illness has hit the village. They haven't the medicine for this strange illness that has hit them. They need help. Now you watch that tent over them. That is you. Watch and you will see yourself." The man saw the people in the village gather together and point around to himself, whom he saw. He could hear them say, "Let's go see that man. Let's turn our lives over to him. Let's see what he can do. We can't do anything else. The chiefs can't help us. The warriors can't help us. Our hunters are sick. The medicine men do not have medicine to help us." This man heard all that. The figures with the man then said, "Watch now." He could see the people go over and talk to him. They said, "It's up to you now. You are going to have to help us. We want to live on. The Great Spirit gave us life and we have been enjoying it. But we are sick now. We might all die. We don't know what to do, so we have come to you."

He heard himself say, "All right. Spread a hide or skin. Spread it down on the ground. Whatever personal property you have that is old or beyond repair, bring from each family." The people did as he requested. He bundled all these things up.

The figures with the man again spoke, "You watch. Watch what you are going to do." The man with the bundle went east where he found a tree. He reached up to one of the limbs and tied the bundle on that limb. Then he turned to the people and told them, "Now go and clean around your lodges. Take out all the ashes, sweep everything and shake everything out. When we get through cleaning, we are going to build a new fire. We are going to be well now."

So this man was watching this performance from the ridge. He saw himself go to his lodge and clean there. The figures with the man then said, "That is you. We are blessing you that you may help your people. Tomorrow those peo-

ple down there are going to get well. They will feel better and they will move on. Now remember that we are blessing you. We picked you out for this." Then the figures sang the fourth song. Afterward, they told the man to go back. He woke up.

Later on, this man's people became sick and he reenacted what he saw in this dream or vision. It all happened. This man cured his people by telling them to clean up their lodges and by building a new fire.

It happened that the next time the people became ill, there was a man among the people who doubted that the first man actually helped his people. When the first man requested the second time that all the people bring items to bundle up, well this "doubting Thomas" brought his best horse wondering what the first man would do with it. He thought that maybe the other would keep the horse. Well, everything happened just as it did before. But the doubting Thomas thinking the man got off lucky the first time, led his horse to this man. But the first man did everything as he did before. He took the bundle and tied it to a tree, and he tied the horse to the tree as well. The camp moved after the people recovered again. In the meantime, doubting Thomas wondered what had happened to the horse. He didn't see it around. Several years later, the people moved back to this old camp. The doubting Thomas then had reason to go in the direction where the first man had tied the horse to the limb. There he found the skeleton of the horse.

"The moral of the story is to live in such a manner that people will not doubt you. That is a true story, a story of my grandfather."

In this story told by Missouria historian and elder Truman Dailey, several points about Otoe-Missouria history are touched upon. It says something about storytelling. It describes an actual epidemic that the people went through. It talks about song compositions, traditional ideas of healing and wellness, and morals and ethics of the people.

There is considerable oral history of tribal people not yet written. Some tribal people do not want their histories written at all, or *in English,* for several reasons. First is the suspicion that they will be appropriated by the larger society like so much other cultural appropriation that has already occurred. Second, the material is often considered sacred and not for the knowledge of outsiders. Third, the "fixed" quality of written histories carries with it some very complex tribal ideas about how this will affect the "living" state of the people and their continuity. Fifth, tribes often fear distortions of their histories. Concerns go on and on.

Those tribes who are open to written histories face some obstacles in preparing them. Any person of tribal descent bent upon familiarizing herself with written history about her tribe in even fairly recent times will have difficulty locating material, unless the tribe has been in the public eye for a number of years. And the amount of recorded history for any particular tribe will always be dominated by a perspective that is external to the tribe itself because these histories come from there.

In reviewing written histories, patterns of interaction between tribal people and the larger society become visible, and these accounts say as much about historians (if not more) as they do the events they relate. Much of the relationship between the larger society and the tribes has been oppressive for tribal societies, and this is emphasized in all literature on indigenous people, although the oppression is not defined this way. Stereotypically, tribes are "conquered," "extinct," "reduced," "insignificant," etc.

Another reason for lack of written tribal histories by tribal people is that it has only been in the last generation that English has been mastered well enough to do this. By force, English has now become the dominant language in many tribal societies. There are, however, a handful of books dealing with tribal histories written in tribal languages. Overall though, suppression of tribal voices has been accomplished through the eradication of their languages. Even tribal histories in English, point up serious discrepancies with American history.

In many tribal societies, to be reliable and credible in interpretation or recall of history is to know and experience, not only rationally, but through the senses and spiritually, individual and group interactions with the rest of the community and the universe as a member of a family, clan, and band.

Tribal histories and historians offer very different perspectives on what happened between tribal societies and the incoming melting-pot society, originating in Europe, when these cultures met and began interaction with one another, compared to what is related in mainstream history. Historical events are also sometimes formally incorporated into communal religious and social activities where they may be reenacted or relived, perhaps similar to the reenactments of historical events by mainstream society. This aspect of tribal history is seen, for example, in the adoption into their annual calendar of a tobacco ceremony between the Pawnees and Wichitas, signifying a shared acknowledgment of a mysterious but important linguistic relationship to one another which neither tribe can explain but which nevertheless links the two people together.

Mainstream literature and history seldom deal seriously with the extinction of great indigenous civilizations that flourished and declined before the Europeans came to the shores of this continent, or even with the extinction of a few groups in historic times. They always begin with the European presence because this is seen as the only significant contribution to the creation of present-day American society. Although mainstream literature and history would have us believe that all Native groups have either been thoroughly assimilated or destroyed since that time, it does not dwell on how this happened. Popular literature about tribal people also seems to be locked into the nineteenth century, where tribes are continually said to have been met, conquered, and ultimately destroyed, all for the sake of a new and better world.

Extinction of some tribal groups did occur as is described in American history. Tribes became extinct in historic times as a result of forced relocation or removal, new diseases and epidemics, warfare, and sometimes by natural catastrophes. The extinction of many tribes beginning in the east and spreading westward coincided with colonization.

As a member of *two* surviving tribal groups, I have been very aware of how close each came to extinction in historic times and what this information meant to the tribes. Because the Otoe-Missouria had always been small, and were always fighting for survival through the centuries, their society was more stable but not unaffected when threatened again in the 1800s. The Pawnees, though, suffered more dramatically when they experienced rapid decline and chaos by a succession of devastating events at that time. For both tribes, therefore, extinction has been a very real possibility over time but particularly in the last two centuries. On a large scale, virtually every tribe in the United States has come face to face with possible extinction, more from manmade than natural causes.

To think that my people might exist no more, after thousands of years upon this continent, has always numbed my senses and brought terror! My reaction to this possibility is a feeling of great and tragic loss of knowledgeable and ancient people who view their way of life and the universe quite unlike any other group. Unless a human being experiences actual extinction, or near-extinction, of her own people, these feelings of terror and loss can never be fully comprehended.

What happened to the Otoe-Missouria and Pawnee Tribes was not very different from what eventually happened to all the tribes that interacted with colonizing groups. Though the relationships between the two sides are often omitted or biased in American history, they are preserved in tribal histories. When these are told by tribal people in formal and informal oral tradition, their content and form, as history, is still discredited and minimized by the mainstream. Because many tribal peoples remain nonliterate in English, the only "real" American language, and they are still uninitiated into a formal Western system of thinking and acting, tribal views of their own experiences and memories are generally received with skepticism and suspicion about the credibility and integrity of tribal people as historians.

The problems with any historical work have to do with substantiating its sources and the integrity of the historians. Historians are highly selective about their focus and perspective. They are also often deemed infallible, above rebuke, in their chronologies and point of view. Undoubtedly, this is more true of written history than oral history because written history is usually regarded as more credible than oral history. Writing fiction as well as nonfiction, some of my concerns about history and historians are seen in my novel, *Ghost Singer.*

David's first draft of the Navajo history was over four hundred pages so far. Of course, he would have to revise and rewrite after he had received his readers' comments on the manuscript. All three readers were historians—and friends. Looking at the manuscript stacked neatly in a box before him, he had to admit that he hadn't written all too much that was new, and the perspective from which he wrote wasn't so radical, either. But his research was impressive, even if he had added nothing new to what other historians already said many times over. And even lacking a unique Navajo perspective in this history, the work would stand on its own merits in the eyes of his colleagues.

Perhaps he had hoped for too much to begin with, because one or two of his colleagues had raised eyebrows at him momentarily, when in great excitement over his own project, he shared his plan to incorporate a unique aspect which would be both critical and timely to his "new" history—a Navajo aspect—which he hoped would enrich the manuscript. The response he received from the two people was not what he expected.

One of them said, "The writing of history is based upon substantiated facts, Dave, of which we have too few for the Navajos. It is sad to say, but nevertheless true, that without records, there is no history. Also, you must take care to remain objective in your work. A history of the scope you suggest would be weakened by any sentimental hogwash which could be construed as romanticism of these people. As a friend, I would advise against taking a Navajo perspective. You're a better historian than that—you don't need it for Christ's sake! What you're suggesting has potential problems for your average reader, need I mention the stuffy historians? Dave, they'll hang you. Don't rock the boat.''

. . .The other colleague was much nicer about David's plan. He said, ''Those people are illiterate, Drake! Let them write their own history when they learn to write and spell. Writing a history from the time of dragons is what you'll be doing. Listen, I've lived here in the Southwest all my life and I know those people. They believe in monsters and half a dozen worlds. People with that background will not have any credibility when it comes to a written history. You'd be jeopardizing your future. . . .''

. . .A long time ago, it was the mountains that had brought David to the Southwest. A long time ago, it was his interest in Pueblo Indians, the Apaches, and the Navajos that brought him here. But at this moment he was just as far away from them as he ever was, no closer to them than the mountains. . . .

. . .When he began this project years ago, he had such high hopes for it. He really intended to add an Indian point of view to the history of this great country. This lofty goal was set by him as a child who was fascinated by Indian people. He took his next step years later.

However, there was an inherent problem in his plan, as he discovered in his adult years. When opportunities to re-write history, so to speak, came his way, he was unprepared. He wasn't Indian and had absolutely no one-to-one relation-ships with Indian people. Consequently, there was no re-source to draw upon which would give him insight into their present existence or their past. The solution was obvious. He would have to find an Indian historian, if there was such a thing.

Along came Willie Begay. . . . Cultivating a relation-ship with Willie was as easy as taking candy from a baby. First of all, David was no slouch as an historian or researcher. Secondly, David did identify with Indian people in some respects; he tended to view Indian people as under-

*dogs in today's world. This was a notion which David kept
deeply hidden from himself.*

*Actually, the reason Willie encouraged the friendship
was not because of David's professional background, or because David fancied himself a do-gooder for the Indian
cause, but because Willie wanted to be involved in the work-
ings of the outside world. To Willie, the real world was the
Navajo world. To David, the real world was history. Willie
crossed back and forth, and the outside world reaffirmed to
him that the Navajo world was real, and he protected it. In
order to do this, he had to be involved in the outside world.*

*In any case, Willie was amiable to David's suggestion
for a Navajo history. This led David to the old man, Jonnie
Navajo, and the illusive search for Navajo slaves.*

*Sitting here now, David realized that at this minute he
really did think it would have been much easier to do without the old man's input. He wouldn't have had to listen to
the old man's long tale, and he wouldn't have had to rethink
his own history of the Navajos. So far, the use of the old man
had only caused a great deal of inconvenience.*

*. . . In the long run, David had decided that his profes-
sional reputation was a life and death matter. This project
was not worth the risks after all. When he had a "real Navajo
history" version in his possession, he could reject it in en-
tirety, or in part, and he could even alter it to suit his needs.
He would take care to be objective, fair, and thorough. He
couldn't think of anyone who could do a better job.*

*David felt better now. His peers could be merciless. He
would do what was necessary to survive.*

*It was true that a long time ago, David had been fasci-
nated by cowboys and Indians. It was also true that a long
time ago, he had wanted to write a real Indian history, but
it was a momentary fancy. Great God in heaven, at one time
David had actually wanted to be one of the Indians. . . . Now
he was grown up. Today, things were as clear to him as the*

> *mountains in the lovely picture before him. He wasn't a cow-*
> *boy or an Indian. He was an historian, a damn good one too,*
> *he thought.*[1]

The histories of my tribes in ancient and historic times always enter into my view of the world, and therefore my writing. It is an element that is sometimes very alien and unfamiliar to some readers. The
history of the United States, as told by mainstream society, and its omission of indigenous peoples, along with its consistently negative images, also deeply affects me. As a tribal person knowledgeable about
my own tribal histories, my writing and perspective defy the cherished
historical American myths about tribal peoples. We were not defeated
and eradicated by the colonizers. We were seriously harmed by them,
but we survived and we live!

Today, my occupation as a writer is related to what my grandfather
and grandmother did when they repeated family history in the manner of their elders, leading the family all over this sacred land, this
continent most recently called America in the last five hundred years,
in their retelling of the Otoe journey from the dawn of time until they
came to rest at Red Rock Creek a little over a century ago. In the same
way, I repeat their words to my children and grandchildren. In tribal
society, this is who history is for, after all, in a very personalized version of time. Receiving and passing on of history is the responsibility of each generation. We are its keepers.

Scholars or authorities from academia, from outside tribal societies, do not necessarily know tribal people best. There is an inherent right of tribal people to interpret events and time in their worlds
according to their own aesthetics and values, as a component of American history, even when this interpretation is different from that of mainstream history.

The history of tribal people on this continent spans more than five
hundred years. My own tribes have been here at least a thousand years.
For these spans of history and prehistory, acknowledgment and gratitude is expressed by the tribes to no one else on the grand scale of
thanksgiving as to their own respective supernatural deities. Even the

people's own ingenious or creative survival skills are not recognized in this manner, let alone those of our so-called conquerors.

For five hundred years, tribal people have lived uneasily side by side with an ever-increasing mainstream population. In this Quincentennial year, we remain strangers to American society and history.

Notes:

1. *Ghost Singer,* pp. 197-200.

Che

A stretch of high empty plains rolled up to touch
the sky in Canada somewhere, a few miles north. The late
summer sky was a pale afternoon blue. Tall yellow grass made scratch-
ing sounds as it was pushed underfoot. Stella wore cowboy boots; they
followed Jim's steps.

"See anything yet?" she asked him in a soft southern drawl.

He shook his head no and raised the cowboy hat on his head back
an inch or two while he chewed on a long stem of grass.

They continued to walk northward in a heavy silence. Their pickup
truck, parked behind them, grew smaller and smaller. They walked
further into the high grass, their legs sinking into it, into the silence
that was magnified out there. The wind occasionally beat the grass
and it rippled, sending wave after wave to Canada.

The landscape looked flat to the two people, but actually they were
climbing a slope. They were in no hurry and took their time. When
the wind pushed on their backs, moving gently north, they didn't re-

---

Che is Otoe for buffalo.

sist. They were guided by it.

Jim turned to Stella and said skeptically, "The old people always say, *This place was black with buffalo once.* I, myself, often wondered."

Stella stopped where she stood and looked around. "You mean right here, Jim?" she asked.

"Yeah," he said, still chewing the long stem. "Our people tell about it all the time. It's an obsession with them I think—the buffalo."

"My people's the same way, Jim. They were like that too. You know, up until two generations ago, they still chased buffalo all through Nebraska. Couldn't seem to forget *che* afterward. I'm not sure they have yet, even with new generations since," she said.

Jim nodded, took Stella's hand. "Hon," he said, "I'll tell you something, a secret I've never told anyone. There have been times when I've doubted that the buffalo and the buffalo people ever existed. I think it was a figment of someone's imagination."

Stella laughed and asked, "Well, are you saying that the 'coming of the whiteman' was a part of that imagination? I mean, after all, he's here."

Their steps carried them further up the slope, following the flow of windy waves that rippled grass northward. Jim spit and said, "You know what I mean. I don't think it's true. I've seen nothing of those times, but the people persistently claim it was so. They tell stories of shaggy, wonderful beasts and tireless people who chased them. Our people sound so childish with those tales. No one takes them seriously anymore. You know the few buffalo I've seen are pitiful creatures over on the protected range. Hard to believe that they're the same ones, the sacred animals the people talk about."

Jim turned toward their vehicle. It was a sliver of metal that gave off such a blinding reflection in the sun that Jim winced.

"Over here somewhere there should be rocks, a line of rocks, if what they say is true. And there should be another on the west rim over there," he pointed. Stella raised her hand to shade her eyes and looked west, just below the sun.

The top of the ridge was still a good distance away. Jim slowed his pace. His eyes scoured the high grass for a hidden line of rocks, but none were visible. He strode in circles for a while, moving the shrubbery and undergrowth with his boots, his search went unrewarded.

"You think everything's gone by now?" Stella asked. The grass danced around her knees under a low, moaning wind. "I mean, you've said before that the last time this particular jump was used was nearly two hundred years ago, didn't you? Is that true?"

"I don't know, except that it was in use for a good five hundred years at least. There should be *something* here." He was almost angry as he said the words. "Damn! I didn't believe it anyway."

The grass undulated southward and then north as he spoke. The wind flapped Stella's long hair over her shoulders, and Jim's shirt collar blew up and touched his ears.

He walked away from Stella and began to stomp the grass down around the thick undergrowth near him. Again he found nothing. Stella stood where she was, trying to imagine the empty plain covered with illusive buffalo.

"There's nothing here," Jim conceded. He *was* angry, she could tell. "Let's head on back," he continued. "It was a figment of someone's imagination. No buffalo, no buffalo people. There's just now. We've never been anything but what we are now."

Jim's anger confused Stella, "Why are you mad, Jim?" she asked with a slight frown.

He answered, "I'm not mad, just disappointed I guess." He yanked his cowboy hat off his head and slapped it against his leg. His shoulder-length hair swirled around his head.

"Do you want to find it Jim, or are you afraid to find it?" Stella asked in a low, barely audible voice.

Jim glared at her. "I'm here, aren't I?" he said, "chasing buffalo that's long gone, or never existed!"

Stella wasn't through talking though. "Maybe we'd rather not know for ourselves if there's anything to all these stories. If we find it, it means the old people know what they've been talking about. It means that life wasn't always what it is now. If we don't find it and this is where it's supposed to be, then the old people are fools perpetuating an older lie that someone started a really long time ago. Either way, it means facing something square in the face."

Jim's expression softened. Looking around him, he answered, "Well, one thing's certain. The earth is as they said—it's beautiful out here. Nothing to stand between you and the Maker. It almost makes me believe there is a Maker somewhere...but I doubt it." The wind tousled his black hair again. He combed it down with his free hand and smashed the hat back on his head.

"Come on," Stella said, "we got time. Let's look around." She held out her hand, and Jim walked to her and put his hand around hers. The two people were simply specks on the land from the distance of their truck.

"You know," she said to Jim after they had walked for some time, "being out here brings back some things I had forgotten since I was a child."

"What's that?" he asked.

"Well, one of my grandmother's names had to do with buffalo. She was a little girl and you know how children are, playing all the time and getting dirty and dusty as quick as they can. My grandmother was like that, I guess. Her girlhood name was Covered With Buffalo Dust. Can you imagine a name like that? Later she took a regular name." Stella frowned as she added, "She's dead now, Jim."

The wind's sound grew, and Jim threw an arm over Stella's shoulders. "There's something else too," the woman told him. "I remember a song about buffalo. It called the buffalo by name. Know what it was?"

Jim shook his head no.

"The song said the buffalo's name was Grandfather. I never understood it," Stella confessed.

Jim didn't answer. He was absorbed in his thoughts. The two moved as one across the earth in solitude. Only the moaning wind spoke.

Unexpectedly Jim found himself studying a broken line of boulders, running south to north, covered with patches of black and orange lichen. He stopped. Stella lifted her boot and rested it on the largest spongy boulder. "You think this is it, Jim?" she asked. Her eyes were strangely lit in excitement.

He didn't answer but followed the line northward. Other boulders lay scattered on both sides of it.

"How does the story go again, Jim?" Stella asked.

"Well, supposedly these walls were to keep the buffalo running in the direction the people wanted them to go. Men were stationed behind them or along them. They say these walls were built up pretty high so the buffalo wouldn't go over them, but had to turn . . . that way." He pointed to the ridge.

Jim and Stella stood there momentarily looking toward the jump. Then she yelled, "I'll race you to it!"

They began to run toward the jump, panting softly, sounding like the wind themselves. In a few minutes they were at the site. Breathlessly she threw herself down on the ground and gasped for air. The land under them dropped abruptly in a deadly fall of several feet. Below that, the earth smoothly folded into a steep ravine.

"Canada begins right there," Jim told her, "where the land meets the sky." He took off his hat again, shook his head, and squashed the hat down on his head once more. The wind grew around them, rustling the tall grass and the clothing they wore. Jim climbed down the drop and began to scout around.

"What are you looking for?" Stella called to him over the wind.

"The place where the holy person stood," he yelled back at her. "He waited below the ridge and it was he who called the buffalo here." His words were tossed in the wind.

Stella pulled herself up and followed. They wandered around until Jim discovered a hollowed out space in the ground, just under the drop. There was a wall of rocks around the indentation. "Here it is," Jim said. He stepped into a space just wide enough for a man to sit or stand.

"What did he do here?" Stella asked.

"I don't really know. Prayed, sang. But he waited here, calling the buffalo over the ridge in some mysterious way. The other people, the hunters, were on top, back there," he pointed up to the ridge. "They got the buffalo to run, to charge as fast as they could, between the line of rocks and men up there. By the time the herd reached the ridge, there was a cloud of dust, and the buffalo fell down here." He pointed again, to the ravine. The wind moaned loudly.

Stella's eyes followed his hand to the spot below them. She was strangely quiet, and so was he after he described the killing. He sat down in the narrow space of the ancient shelter. When she saw that he wasn't going to budge for a while, she walked toward the ravine.

The wind calmed in the jagged ravine, a dramatic contrast to the moaning on the hill. Stella made her way through the abundant brush and found herself in a small clearing. Bright-colored pebbles were generously scattered over the earth. She looked up to Jim, still holding the same position. His eyes narrowed and focused toward Canada.

Stella took off the cowboy shirt she wore over her T-shirt. She threw it down on the ground and sat on it. Then she pulled off one boot at a time. She lay down on one arm and looked back up toward Jim, wondering what he was thinking. He had not moved. The sun was poised on the hill southwest of Jim, while puffs of clouds sailed over the ridge to Canada.

She lay in a fold of the earth. The brush encircling the clearing made noises as birds dove into it. Peace and quiet reigned where hundreds of buffalo once fell. That thought stayed with her. She wanted to close her eyes.

Several minutes elapsed with Jim still lost in his own reverie. He paid no attention to Stella.

She dreamed of thunder rolling over her. Of dark clouds blown from the earth up to the sky. Of choking, blinding dust, and a hot, charging wind. A rumbling on the ridge above Jim. He'd called them with a name. The cloud on the ridge emitted a thundering sound and the earth trembled. She felt it beneath her bones.

Jim shook her. He said, "Let's go back. There's nothing here."

Startled, she sat up and looked around. The jump was quiet, the earth so still.

"Jim," she said, "I had a strange little sleep. I dreamed of something coming, no running, to the edge of the jump up there. Buffalo, I think. *Che.* I never saw them, but they were so close that I heard them and felt them. I think I even smelled them."

She began to pull her boots on while Jim said, "It's your imagination. This place got to you, that's all."

She shook her shirt and put it back on. "Jim," she insisted, "I could swear there were buffalo here!"

Jim spread his arms to indicate the space around him, "Do you see anything?"

Stella shook her head and said, "No, but that doesn't mean much. I was going to look around before I went to sleep. I'm not ready to go yet." She hurried away from Jim and disappeared into the brush.

Jim decided to humor her and waited patiently, sitting in the dirt and tossing pebbles at the birds diving into the brush. She returned in a few minutes. Jim asked her, "Find anything?"

Her answer was no. They began to climb back up toward the jump. They took a different route than the one they had followed down. Stella's eyes stayed on the ground, seeking a fragment of time, of something old and hidden that only they could spot.

"Look, I didn't know you were going to be fanatic about this," Jim laughed.

Stella replied, "I guess I might be silly at that. It's just that they were so close, I could feel their breath. It felt like the wind."

The heel of her boot caught itself in the cracked ground. She lifted her leg, and the heel imprint was stamped in the sandy wash. Then it sifted slowly into the earth. She knelt down to scratch the dirt with her fingernails. Jim watched her, entranced by her new behavior.

"It's here!" she told him excitedly.

"What?" he asked calmly.

"Bones," she said, "they're underneath."

Jim wore an amused expression. "You're kidding!" he said.

"No," she answered, her fingers digging rapidly, throwing dust. She dug for several minutes until her hands were bruised and scratched, and dusty to the wrists. She brushed dirt from a smooth white porous surface that appeared.

"There!" she said. She stopped digging and looked up at Jim. His expression was hard to read. "See Jim, there's buffalo here!" She twisted her hair back when it began to fly around her face and left a streak of dirt on her forehead and chin.

Jim laughed at her, and himself, chasing buffalo this way. Stella understood and laughed too. She added, "Buffalo people, too!"

Jim pulled her up, threw an arm over her shoulder, and guided her toward the rim of the jump. At the top they surveyed the ravine again. Stella turned to Jim. Before she could speak, Jim said to her, "You're all dusty."

She answered, "It's buffalo dust, Jim. We're all buffalo dust. I finally understand."

Jim asked, "Understand what?"

"The song," she said. The wind moaned everywhere. "The buffalo people live on Jim. The buffalo may be gone or may be penned up on some protected range. But their bones and ours are the same. That's why the people keep the buffalo alive. Feed the stories of *che* to us."

"When I was sitting down on the ledge where the holy person sat," Jim responded. "I had a strange feeling that if I called the buffalo here, they would come. I had a silly urge to try. But then I didn't know what to say and the feeling went away. I guess it's the buffalo man in me. I didn't know it was there." He laughed.

The two people turned and began their trek to the pick-up truck. It was a long way. The sun was setting on them and the buffalo jump.

Stella turned to Jim. The plain was still, without a ripple of wind then. "It's beautiful here," she said, "but you know what's best of all about this?"

Jim gave a parting look at the jump and did not answer.

Stella answered her own question. "That it exists. Amid the skyscrapers, space shuttles, the computers. This place exists untouched and will, as long as we hide it and remember that it's here."

Jim was absorbed in his own thoughts. He turned to Stella and said, "*This place was black with buffalo once.*" He waved his hand over the plain. As they walked to the truck, she answered, "*che.*" It echoed in the silence there.

Part Four
Identity

Many years have passed since I first heard the voice of oral tradition at my ear, the cadence of words resembling drumbeats coming from along the creek. It has been about forty years since I first sought the source of that mysterious and mystical voice, and began a journey which led me here.

Many years have passed since my childhood when I envisioned a world entirely Indian, never expecting, in my childish dreams, for it to be disrupted, or gone, or replaced by a foreign intrusion that was extremely detrimental, dangerous, and overpowering to me.

Many years have passed since the experiences of living in a larger society that denied tribal existence and worth converged upon the child that I was, leaving me dazed, scarred, and hurting.

All my life has been spent figuring out exactly where I fit into patterns and networks of relationships that already existed, laid out long before I was born. Most of my responses to these patterns and relationships have been intuitive rather than learned in the classroom, such as resistance to joining the mainstream. Protection of my individuality and right to the personal expression of what and who I am were always priorities. At the same time, it was a struggle to resist the most confining pigeon-holes into which Indian people, women, and writers are stuffed, and to escape those that snuff out will and creativity.

Finding a place in today's world meant differentiating personal and tribal values from those of mainstream society. Not until my late teens and early twenties did I realize that there was a *choice* in how much to give of myself to that world. No longer was I the small child in boarding or public school whose life was out of her control, manipulated by forces larger than she was, placed on the assembly line of a massive machine that would shape and mold me into something unfamiliar or repellant to myself and other tribal people.

When I made this distinction, my birthright as a tribal person in the twentieth century became clearer. It restored my sense of well-being, personal and tribal history, and a promising, intact future as well. A personal vision of myself, compatible with what I earlier knew life to be, returned the very first picture I held as a child—the universe from the banks of Black Bear and Red Rock Creeks. Miraculously, it was whole again, and it became that much more valuable to me.

All these experiences had everything to do with becoming a writer, and my identity as a tribal person and a woman shapes and inspires the words I've since written.

* * *

Over the years I have explored relationships with other people around me, including those very close to me, like my mother and grandmother. My life has been different from theirs, but our experiences as women and tribal people have been inherently the same.

My Pawnee grandmother was born some fifty years before me. Although she was from Indian Territory, she was the link between Oklahoma and Nebraska. She was reared as an orphaned child, without a mother. Her father was a member of the Pitahauerat band who in Indian Territory, went by the English name of Captain Jim.

In accordance with tribal custom, Captain Jim had several plural marriages. These were unions where he married two or more sisters at the same time or successively. Most of his wives died from new diseases introduced to the tribes in Nebraska and Oklahoma. This was the social environment into which my Grandma Cora was born. Her mother was called Jennie by the whites.

My grandmother was married twice in her lifetime. Her second marriage was to my mother's father, who came from a rich background. He was the son of a Pawnee man whose English name was Robert Taylor. Grandma's second marriage produced three children, and my mother was the middle child.

My mother, like her mother, grew up with one parent, for her father died when she was only a couple of years old. But the difference between her and my grandmother is rather astonishing. Her command of the Pawnee language is extremely limited and her knowledge of Pawnee culture is almost nonexistent. But she knows more about both than she admits. There is even a great contrast between her and her older sister, my aunt, who is a fluent Pawnee speaker and a learned elder in Pawnee culture. Of course, the differences between them are the result of their individual experiences with the institutions of the predominant society, e.g. school and Christianity.

How my grandmother, mother, and I have lived has been influenced by the time into which we were born, and the impact of the cultures with which we have interacted upon us. No doubt the Pawnee tribal-federal relationship has touched us all in a very deep, complex way. An example of this is the fact that the three of us each attended the same boarding school that was provided by the Treaty of 1857 in exchange for Pawnee land. Having mothered children and grandchildren, we also shared these experiences. Our views of Pawnee traditional teachings and our various experiences have both brought us closer together and sometimes separated us. Our economic status in the larger society has generally been low. Our status as acknowledged members of the Pawnee tribe has always been high, though we each found our places in different ways.

Through this look back to Grandma Cora, and even further back to the time of Captain Jim and Robert Taylor and their spouses, I have been able to see the earth lodges of the Pawnees, the villages beside the Platte River (in Nebraska), and know that these homes and people exist within me. These people and places are reflected in my writing because they reinforce my identity. And since we are all uniquely ourselves, my stories and other writings are always a little different from theirs and other peoples', even other Indian writers.

All literature is created from material such as this. Out of the desire to express memory and experience individually in each generation, another voice is given to it, a voice both inclusive and exclusive of oral tradition, one that picks up *after* the pause of oral tradition and carries on the story of particular tribes and what life is in that generation. I did not recognize, at first, that I gave my voice to the story. *I did not recognize my own voice* because it had been hushed for a time.

My stories and other writings are a counterpart, therefore, to the voice of oral tradition *and* to all literature with which I have come into contact since I first drew breath. I write for tribal people more than any other group.

My writing encompasses many issues and topics in both fiction and nonfiction. In the cultures by which I am most affected, creativity is understood to be inherent in being human and resourceful. Expressing creativity is a facet of being alive. Through my writing activities, I have been able to grow in ways that I did not dream possible years ago.

This growth is the subject of much of my writing now, growth as a woman, a human being of a particular family, and growth in understanding my connection with the universe, my Bear and Buffalo Clan relationship to it. Because I have become a grandmother, I find myself writing about grandchildren and time.

The grandmother sat now on the edge. Her skinny legs dangled above the floor. Forever, her grandchild's mind froze the picture it took of the unblinking eyes of her grandmother, who tentatively stood holding onto the bed for a minute and a couple of minutes more. She wore a long, loose, light gown that lit her skin in a pale luminous glow. She was a wisp of light moving across the room.

"Come here," she said to her grandchild standing on

the bed. The small girl dropped the doll and slid down to the floor. Again, the grandchild froze the memory as she stood and looked up at her grandmother's face with white glowing hair pouring down a shoulder to her.

The grandmother's feet—brown, old, and rough— glided across the smooth floor. "Come on, little one," she said, looking down at the tiny figure following her. "Let's dance. Just us. I'll teach you. That way when everything else is gone, you'll have this."

The tiny figure allowed herself to be pulled. Her feet, with one painted toenail, stepped wherever the grandmother's went. The grandchild tried to move her small body exactly as the grandmother did.

The room filled with peels of laughter escaping from the tiny figure as she stepped on her grandmother's toes, or into her heels. The movement of the two figures rippled around the room in a soft and rhythmic glow.

"Grandma!" the tiny figure exclaimed between bursts of bell-like laughter. And it seemed to the grandmother that more light and air entered the room. Suddenly she was outdoors, in the time of long ago, when she was a child too, following her own grandmother's dancing feet across the ground. For a moment, she felt strong and good.

But too quickly, the grandmother tired and returned to bed. Her grandchild found the doll again. The room dimmed and quieted a little, but for the glow of golden light coming from the grandchild and the grandmother in the bed, and for the very few words that needed to be said. [1]

In sisterhood and brotherhood we find refuge and tolerance and love for the human condition. Sisterhood is always an aspect of my writing: sisterhood to all female principles in the universe; sisterhood tribe to tribe, in the broadest sense. But this does not preclude writing about brotherhood because the guiding vision in both tribes I represent emphasizes balances.

Sisterhood is seen in the story, "The International Bridge," when the character Irma meets another Indian woman in a Mexican border town and learns that the political border separating the two is a line that can become insignificant, even lost, in the shifting sands of the desert. The two women are clearly in tune with one another. Irma tells the woman:

> *"You remind me of my grandmother. She's a lot like you. She wears the same look when she talks about her children and grandchildren. And, also like you, she is not well."*
> *The old woman looked very seriously at Irma. Her brown eyes met Irma's head on.*
> *"Your eyes are the same as hers, too. And they are the eyes of a Mayan girl I recently met in Canada...."*[2]

Besides examining relationships with one another as human beings, I also try to look, with tribal eyes, at the human relationship with the land and the universe. In the novel *Ghost Singer,* this becomes evident when the character Wilbur Snake is outside alone one winter day.

> *Although the sun shone brightly, a dusting of snow lay on the hills and in the valleys. The snow was hard, burning cold to the touch, and had dusted the hills for nearly a week. Wilbur stood inside the chicken-wire fence, under ice-covered trees, feeding a couple of dozen chickens. When he was done, he walked back to the house and sat down in one of the chairs outside. He wanted to feel the coldness of the snow and the sun. It was directly in front of him, but it gave no warmth today, only flat light. Wilbur squinted under its glare and against the bright snow. A strong wind blew at him, and he pulled his jacket a little tighter around himself. The woolen cap made his forehead itch and he wrinkled his brow as he gazed at the frozen earth around him.*
> *No matter what season of the year, Wilbur was an outdoor man. He had to come face-to-face with the outdoors*

*on a daily basis or he didn't feel alive. He needed to feel
alive. As the wind slapped his face now, Wilbur needed it.
When his hearing was better, he loved to listen to the wind
moan and whisper to him. At times he could still hear it,
and he hugged it to him as often as he could, as much as
the wind embraced him.*

*All his life he'd made a study of viewing the four direc-
tions from this place. He felt the knee-high grass ripple
around his legs for the rest of the year and welcomed the
crunch of it under his boots or in his hands. He knew the
water around here by its many colors, the dirt at his feet by
touch, taste, and smell. All of these things spoke to Wilbur
in a language that only he could decipher and understand.*

*And there was much to be said on this clear, blistery-
cold winter day. Wilbur listened to the silent screaming sun,
the burning cold crusty snow, and the ice-filled creeks running slow as suspended time. The wind was snakelike this
morning, whipping one way and then another, and curling
itself around Wilbur. He could see it move over the land in
spiral dips by the movement of the trees and the flurry of
ice sifting through the air in little crystals.*

*He gave himself over to the winter, as he gave himself
over to countless endless scorching summers. He saw himself as a real part of each season. Like the bent tree nearest
the house, he had come through the seasons with it, with
the tall grass and the other life here. They had shared the
same space and time in a way that two human beings could
not share the same things. In essence, the out-of-doors
brought much comfort and knowledge to Wilbur, and an
awareness of the delicate relationship of all things to one
another out there. It met him on different terms than those
set by his fellow men. In the bitterest cold and hottest days,
he still found that out here, facing the wind, he was most
alive, the most exhilarated. And out here, there was nothing to block his connection with other life surrounding him.*

He became an extension of the wind, of the trees, of the land,
and the sun. He could sit here forever. He might sit here
forever.

Not even Anna, or his children, Junior and the other
child that had died long ago, took the place of what he found
out here. They could not. His relationship to the universe,
the world, was for infinity. His relationship to human be-
ings was more temporal. [3]

In my stories, landscapes are as important as the characters because I have learned that human beings tend to be extensions of whatever "landscape" (physical, natural, artificial) they are in. Sometimes
these backgrounds are obscure and not clearly defined. This was the
case in the story "Mythomania." [4] The nature of myths in all societies is that they are obscure and hard to pin down. In this story, the
protagonist Firefly is very much a product of the myths surrounding
him. Into the obscurity of these myths, Firefly also eventually recedes
after he fails to accomplish what he set out to do in the story. The landscape comsumes him.

At other times in my stories it is very clear that the landscape is
a part of the people, or that *they* are the landscape, or the landscape
is a map of their own visions and experience. When Lydia loses one
of her legs in "The Sun Is Not Merciful," she says of its absence:

"Ah miss my leg, Bertha. Ah miss my ankle and my toes
and my toenails, too. Sometimes it feels like it's still there,
but ah look at it and ah don't see it and ah know that it must
not be there. Ah'm gonna miss it bad, Bertha. Don't seem
right to go through life having to throw away one shoe each
time you buy a new pair." [5]

She is speaking about a part of herself that has been severed and
pulled from her, the land and its origins.

Through stories such as these, a tribal writer is able to describe
a part of American experience that mainstream society and literature

do not include. And very importantly, she is also able to carry on a timeless dream and vision of tribal people that has a place in contemporary society.

From Black Bear and Red Rock Creeks is where I speak, though I am often not physically there. The teachings of tribal oral traditions are what call me back time and again. There, the silences that are the counterpart to the spoken words and sounds of life are deep and profound. After the words, the stories, and the songs, always come silence we are told. The spaces of silence are given to ponder all the mysteries of the universe and our own existence in relation to the mystery of the whole. When the silence eventually moves us to speak, we know the power of silence and our own words. *Remember both, we are told.*

Notes:

1. "Grass in a High Wind" (unpublished short story).

2. "The International Bridge" (unpublished short story).

3. *Ghost Singer,* pp. 201-202.

4. *The Sun Is Not Merciful,* pp. 27-37.

5. "The Sun Is Not Merciful," p. 125.

The Web

It was a season of descending spiders, of transparent webs strung everywhere. First the webs draped only the bushes outside Hilda's small house, but day by day the spiders extended their reach, their silky threads, taking them closer to her home.

Hilda saw them creep toward her. When sunlight illuminated the bushes, layer upon layer of webs encircled them, knit together in sticky chains of multicolored hues. They clung tightly to the branches, undisturbed by the early morning wind.

Hilda stood among the bushes in streaming sunlight with her long, dark hair flying around her face. She poked a web with an index finger and searched the layers for the threads belonging to that particular one. Slowly she extricated it, a large, springy, loose web twice the width of her hand, with two dried butterfly wings flapping in the threads. Hilda blew on the web. Its long stringy fibers stretched and expanded, then bounced back into the original loose, diamond-shaped pattern.

Hilda turned around. The bushes behind her were smothered with webs the color and texture of cotton after their long exposure to the wind and sun. Hilda smoothed her hair down from the blowing wind and knotted it at the back of her head.

Then she noticed the spiders moving upon her house. Overnight the spiders took over and draped intricate threads on the door hinges and windows; webs hung thickly on the screens. Hilda had never seen anything like this season of spiders in all her forty years. She frowned and wondered what the appearance of spiders in such numbers meant.

She opened the front door, brushing away several long spider threads from it, one with a spider dangling at the end. "Shoo," she said, as she tried to throw the threads away, but they clung to her rough fingers. She wiped the threads on her worn dress, then went inside and put on a dark apron and wrapped a red scarf around her head. The turban brought out her honey-colored eyes, very old eyes for a middle-aged woman. Hilda always had old eyes, even as a child. Her eyes went to a broom in the corner of the kitchen, its straws broken and frayed at the end.

She carried the broom outside to remove the spider webs from the door and windows. Hilda went all around the house, sweeping away each web methodically with the broom. They were everywhere. Before she was done, webs hung on her clothes, her nose, and trailed off her turban to her shoulders.

As she lifted the broom over a window she spoke to the spiders, then invisible in the ground and the cracks of the house. "I know you can hear me," she said. "You and me have always gotten along. We haven't ever fought one another. So, why is it that you've now moved in on me like this? I don't understand it, do you hear? I don't understand you any more." Her words were blown away by the morning wind.

When she was through cleaning the windows, she went back inside to dress for work. She pulled the webs from herself and changed her clothes. Then she started the short walk to the cafe where she was employed.

She followed a narrow path, keeping her eyes on the ground as she strolled through the woods. A variety of insects shared the trail, creeping back and forth, and then two rabbits appeared. One of them stared at her curiously before moving on. Spider webs hung on the tree limbs along the path. She stopped momentarily to study them. Hundreds of webs were scattered everywhere. Suddenly, a limb dropped from above and hung eye-level before her. She nearly jumped out of her skin! A large web, several inches wide and half as long, silky in the light, was draped in the fork of the limb. The web was suspended in mid-air. Next, a spider jumped from above, landing and balancing on one of the elastic threads, a large menacing spider with luxuriant furry legs and a hard black body. Hilda blinked at the creature. Its intricate web had already trapped several smaller insects. One kicked and twisted in the gooey threads. Hilda walked around the web and went on.

The cafe was empty, though it smelled of brewed coffee and bacon. She was a few minutes late. No one noticed except the bleary-eyed waitress whom Hilda was to replace.

"Morning," Hilda said. "Long night?"

"Not as long as some," the other woman answered. "Lots of truckers."

"Go on home now, Lou," Hilda said. She stored her sweater and purse under the counter and slipped into the ladies room to put on a light green waitress uniform. When she returned, Lou hadn't moved from the table yet.

"Sit down here, Hilda," Lou said. "Everything's clean and done. Tables, counters, windows, salt shakers, ketchup bottles, everything."

"Have you noticed that spiders are everywhere?" Hilda asked, making idle conversation, and pouring herself a glass of water.

"What spiders?" Lou answered. "Where? Maybe we should call the exterminators."

"Not in here," Hilda laughed. "Just everywhere else. My house for instance."

"Oh," Lou shrugged. "Can't say that I have. . ."

"It's real funny," Hilda said. "No, I don't mean funny."

"Do you know what your problem is, Hilda?" Lou asked with a tired raised eyebrow. You're always thinking like an Indian. Always noticing things like how many spiders there are all of a sudden. You have to stop doing that. There's no place for that kind of thinking in the world anymore. Nowadays, there are exterminators for those things. We don't have to notice spiders and such anymore, if we don't want to." She laughed good-naturedly.

"I don't want to hurt your feelings, Hilda," Lou continued, "but someone has to be direct about this. This is how things are today. I used to be like you. I'd try to read signs, watch the earth and sky. But I learned they don't matter anymore." She patted Hilda's shoulder and laughed again.

"Don't laugh at me," Hilda said seriously. "Something's going on. I just don't know what it is though."

"Ask them what's happening then," Lou said with a teasing snicker. She rubbed her bleary eyes.

"I did," Hilda confessed.

"For pete's sake, Hilda!" Lou answered unbelievingly. "Are you still doing all those silly things? Better not let anyone around this cafe know that. Why, they'll say you're crazy."

A customer entered the cafe and Hilda went to serve him. She returned a few minutes later and asked Lou, "How come you're still hanging around? Aren't you tired?"

Lou nodded. "No ride home today. My daughter is using my car. But Ben will pick me up soon."

Lou went to take off her uniform. When she came back, she joined Hilda at the table. "Are you afraid of spiders?" she asked Hilda. Hilda shook her head no.

"Now me, *I am*," she said. "One went into my ear when I was a little girl. I swear it felt just like a dinosaur walking around inside my head. I heard each footstep that monster took. It nearly drove me up the wall."

"What did you do?" Hilda asked.

"I held my head underwater until the spider came out. I was O.K. It didn't bite me or anything like that. But it was an experience I don't ever want to repeat. For sure, I don't want any more spiders going into my ears!" She laughed and shuddered.

Lou kept Hilda company until her husband arrived.

Hilda worked her eight hours and started home. There were no electric lights between her house and the cafe. She walked quickly through the path filled with evening silence. Only her footsteps could be heard. The trees looked thicker and more numerous to Hilda in the twilight.

Eventually she came out of the woods and turned to her little house sitting alone in the last streak of twilight. Her door was barely visible. A few feet from the door was a metal can with a lid where Hilda stored odds and ends. She opened the lid and triumphantly pulled out a flashlight. She turned it on, but the batteries were dead. She dug in the metal can again. "Aha!" she said, and pulled out a package of flashlight batteries.

Hilda shined the light into her purse until she found the house key, then she turned the flashlight on the doorknob, the keyhole. She gasped. Carefully, she raised the light and shined it on the door. Layers of webs completely blocked her entry into the house. She began to wipe the webs away with her fingers. Finally, she unlocked the door.

She pushed it open and stepped inside. The only light in the house came from her hand. Spiders scurried across the floor and walls as Hilda entered, holding the flashlight before her. They were everywhere, in all sizes and shapes. After a couple of seconds, the spiders disappeared into the cracks of the house and into the cracks of Hilda's mind.

She lit the house in electric power and put candles here and there in the darker places. They gave off a faint odor of wax, vanilla, and flame. She changed into a long white nightgown and freed her long hair. She made tea and built a small fire in the black cast-iron stove sitting in the center of the house. First she tried to mend some clothes, but after a while she put the sewing box away. She threw the clothes on the bed. Then she tried to read. She flipped through the shiny pages of half a dozen magazines, only to find that her mind kept wandering away. That happened with the needle and thread too. The stitching reminded her of the spiders that had invaded her home.

The fire was reassuring and warm; lights blazed in every part of the house.

"Time to think, Hilda, old girl," Hilda said, looking around the room. "Time to think. Even if it is 'like an Indian' as Lou says." Her old eyes looked up at the ceiling. Webs hung up there, too, in the corners of the room.

"What do I know about spiders?" she asked herself. She thought and thought, but no answers came.

"I don't know anything about spiders," she conceded after half an hour, "nothing at all!"

She got up to tend the fire, stir the coals and add two logs, then huddled in the rocking chair once more. "I'm not thinking like an Indian at all," she said with a sigh. "I doubt they would ask such a stupid question!" She frowned and said, "Hilda, old girl, you're on your own here, the only Indian around. This is between you and the spiders. You *know* they're here for a reason."

She tried to think logically about the invasion of the spiders but only confused herself. She felt webs in her brain. Her head pounded, and she closed her eyes.

As she slept in the rocking chair, her feet propped on the footstool, the spiders came out into the light in one grand sweep of motion. They scurried across the ceiling, floor, and walls. Some moved jerkily, inch by inch. Others jumped from place to place; a few crawled elegantly on long feathery legs. In the corners of the room the spiders began to weave circles and squares into complex, intricate webs.

Underneath the rocker, several spiders crawled up the chair. In a few minutes they disappeared into the folds of Hilda's nightgown. A couple crossed her bare arm. Hilda swiped at the spiders in her sleep, but she did not wake. Another hung on a long loose strand of hair. It made its way to the top of Hilda's head, circled the crown a couple of times, until it let itself down to skirt across her face. It had no weight, and Hilda did not feel it at all as it traveled to her ear and settled there on the lobe. For the rest of the night, it stayed in this place.

Hilda had several dreams. First the elders came, dressed in gray. They walked in circles around her chair. They were men and women, a parade of ancient faces gesturing at the webs in the corners of the room. They tenderly smoothed her long hair around her sleeping face

as if she were a child. They held her hand, bent and kissed her forehead, and stirred the coals in the stove. Then they covered her with
a blanket and blew out the candles as they departed. Other indecipher-
able dreams came and went throughout the night.

Hilda heard a whisper at her ear. The voice was small. Hilda
strained to hear.

"Grandchild," the voice said, "Grandchild!"

Hilda tried to answer, but no sound came out of her mouth. She
tossed her head and lifted a hand, but it dropped quickly, heavy and
limp.

"Sleep, Grandchild," the voice said, "but listen as you sleep. Listen as you sleep."

Hilda's troubled face smoothed.

"I've a story to tell," the distant voice said. "But do not listen with
your ears and mind. Listen with your hands, listen with your feet, listen
with your skin and hair."

Hundreds of spiders were poised on the rocking chair, spinning
silky threads around Hilda, dressing her in webs. She heard them with
her feet, hands, skin, and hair. Their sticky webs wrapped her in a
shimmering cocoon on the rocking chair.

The spiders worked all night. In the morning hours, they completed their task and abandoned Hilda and the rocking chair. Hilda
was covered with sparkly threads, webs were draped over the arms
of the chair. Hilda felt the spiders depart.

Again the voice whispered in her ear, "Grandchild," it said, "take
care."

Hilda tossed again. The spider ran quickly down her nightgown,
leaving no trail.

She opened her eyes and looked up. The lights were bright around
the house. She looked down at her nightgown. Layers of iridescent
threads circled her hips and breasts. She brushed them off and rubbed
her arms and hands.

The house was quiet, no spiders were anywhere. Outside, the sky
was getting light.

Hilda turned off all the light switches and moved from the chair to her bed. She sprawled on top, face down, expecting to be asleep again in seconds. Sleep didn't come. After a while, she turned over and searched the ceiling. This time her old eyes deeply probed the webs up there.

"Maybe I've been looking at this all wrong," she whispered. "It's not the spiders at all . . . ."

She began to think back to when the spiders first appeared.

Several months before, Edith first entered Hilda's life. Edith who always left a slick trail of sweet words dripping continually from her mouth! Edith of the pincher-grip on those caught in the intricate webs she spun for her victims.

Hilda and Edith met at Hilda's old job, another cafe across town. Edith was Hilda's boss. Hilda had seen a Help Wanted sign in the cafe window and had gone inside and applied for the job. Edith, herself, hired Hilda.

At the beginning, it seemed that Hilda and Edith were a lot alike, even down to their appearances. Both were alone, in middle age, and they had grown children. There were other similarities too. As the weeks passed though, differences between the two began to surface like growing clouds on a sunny horizon. These were big differences in Hilda's mind.

Right from the start, Hilda had been uneasy as Edith invaded her life. It seemed as if Edith moved into it overnight, taking over and taking charge. She began by scheduling all of Hilda's time during work hours and after. She demanded to know everything about Hilda's life, even the deep, dark secrets. *She especially wanted to know the deep, dark secrets.* Earlier, Edith had been subtle about this, but later all traces of subtlety disappeared. Along with this information, Edith asked about every thought that Hilda ever had.

"What are you thinking right now?" Edith asked with a sweet, innocent, look that convinced Hilda she was genuinely interested.

Hilda was flattered the first week or so by this newfound attention. But being asked the same question repeatedly, day after day, several times a day, began to affect Hilda in a strange way. She began to protect and guard her feelings and thoughts. She didn't want Edith to poke at them all the time. She pulled back from Edith then.

That was when Hilda noticed that Edith skillfully manipulated almost everyone who came into contact with her. Edith poked at all of them, pulling their intestines, hearts, and souls out of them and into herself. Edith fed upon these things; she grew large and powerful while her victims wilted and died in her pincherlike hands.

Edith knew everything there was to know about the waitresses and waiters who worked under her supervision. Furthermore, she took pride in possessing this dubious knowledge. After she prodded their secrets from them, Hilda saw her use these against her co-workers, holding their secrets over them like a scepter to manipulate and bind them to her. The secrets that were spilled to Edith in moments of weakness became her power. With these, she pulled strings and made everyone dance.

This was not enough for Edith, though. She demanded loyalty from her workers, and other things, including favors and invitations to private family gatherings. She also told everyone how to live, and because she knew the secret things she did, each person in her web had little choice but to sit through all of Edith's lectures as she patiently explained why he or she was the way he or she was.

Whenever Edith spoke, she cast a strange spell upon those who heard. She wore the perfect guise of maternal love. She looked far away and thoughtfully spoke in sweet words about her victim's strength and fortitude, warm beating heart, and illusive soul. Hilda quickly learned that this performance was misdirection and that it was how Edith conned everyone into her net. At Edith's most eloquent moments, she was the ultimate figure of trust. Hilda, herself, had fallen under Edith's hypnotic spell more than once. Everyone believed Edith for a while; they believed her words of syrup and her wide, ever-present, forced smile.

Hilda successfully avoided Edith for a few days, but then Edith approached her. She wore a broad smile. She hugged Hilda tightly, sizing her up before she spoke. "You must be ill," Edith suggested, because Hilda had withdrawn from her.

Hilda nodded. "Could be," she agreed. But to herself she asked,

Because I don't want to see you anymore? She let Edith's remark go.

The more Hilda pulled away, the more Edith darted and jumped after her. Edith called her "moody" in a teasing, challenging way. She was persistent, darting after Hilda all the time. Hilda was slippery, not quite yet all the way into her web. In one last mighty effort, Edith, with her sweet words and viselike grip, tried to pry Hilda's mouth open to extract her thoughts, her deep, dark secrets, her intestines, her heart and soul. Hilda resisted. She clenched her teeth and rolled her fists while Edith studied Hilda analytically and tried her best to read Hilda's mind.

The situation became more serious. Edith began to interrogate Hilda about her activities from sunrise to sunset, and those times in between. Hilda played along for a while but then caught herself sounding like the six o'clock news report. One day, she abruptly stopped giving the reports, without apology or explanation. This set Edith on edge. She circled Hilda. Around and around and around again she went, trying to find the right words to bring Hilda closer to her.

Edith went to Hilda's home and investigated things there. Hilda stood passively in the corner, feeling like a stranger while Edith walked through the rooms, picking up objects here and there to admire or criticize before setting them down again.

She met Hilda's children, twin girls and a son. Hilda, with increasing fear and alarm, watched Edith move in on them so fast that they never knew what had hit them. In a matter of a couple of hours, Edith had pulled everything out of them, their most vital organs, and she laid these like trophies around the room. Hilda's children were drained and tired but were still under Edith's enchantment. Confused, wan, and shaken by the interlude with Edith, Hilda led them away, vowing to never again hand them over, even grown as they were, to Edith again. Hilda shuddered and watched Edith depart, rosier and bigger than ever, plumped up and energized on Hilda's children.

A showering of gifts from Edith occurred next. This unexpected show of affection toward Hilda made her all the more uneasy. With a deepening dread, she decided to speak to Edith about this behavior and all the other things that made her uncomfortable. She spoke to

Edith about their relationship over coffee one day.

"I'm uneasy with our relationship," she said, carefully selecting her words. "I don't want to hurt your feelings, but I must express myself. I don't like having to tell you every day what is on my mind, and about every little thought I have. I won't give reports to you anymore on what I do, or on who I see. I won't give my children to you so that you can pry into their lives. I think that all these things you are asking of me, and of all of us who work here, are too much."

She waited for Edith's response. One moment, then two, passed. Tears filled Edith's eyes. "I thought you were my friend," she said in a sob.

"I think I am," Hilda answered. "I've tried to be. I give you friendship, Edith, not ownership."

Edith looked wounded, as if no one had ever said such a thing to her.

"And please, no more gifts," Hilda said lastly. "Do you understand that gifts are not necessary?" Edith still sobbed into a napkin.

From that moment on, Edith became more spiderlike. She became sweeter and more syrupy, if that was possible.

Hilda was due a salary increase after ninety days, but by then the relationship with Edith had come apart. She wasn't too surprised when Edith informed her, in a tone of sad, sisterly compassion, that the restaurant had decided to let Hilda go if Hilda didn't agree to extend her trial period a little longer. Hilda nodded and bit her lip thoughtfully. She has risked this all along. She took off her apron and went home. She did not go back again, not even to pick up her last pay check.

She thought that that would be the last of Edith. But less than a week later, Edith showed up at Hilda's house with Hilda's final paycheck. Hilda opened the door, at the same time blocking the entrance to the house.

"Aren't you going to invite me inside?" Edith asked, "to thank me for bringing this to you?"

"Thank you," Hilda said. "Now please go."

She closed the door. Edith yelled through it. "I don't understand you, Hilda. After all I've done for you—hiring you the way I did, giving you all those nice things, and this is the thanks I receive!" She was angry, but a few seconds later she was tearful again. "I just wanted you to be my friend!"

Hilda went into her bedroom and turned up the radio. Finally, Edith went away. Temporarily.

Hilda found herself another job. After two months, Edith came into the new cafe where Hilda worked. Edith and Hilda apologized to one another. They agreed to start over, to be more tolerant of one another. In less than four weeks, Edith was dropping by to see Hilda every other day for a few minutes. Over coffee and donuts, or a hamburger and fries, Edith's interrogations began.

"What are you thinking, honey?" Edith asked with a sweet smile. Hilda was wary. She noticed something new added then. Edith already knew what Hilda had done and who she had seen *before* Hilda gave the reports. A dark cloud entered Hilda's mind again.

Twice in the past two weeks, Hilda ran into Edith in the most unexpected places. It was almost as if Edith was following and watching her. Hilda found herself shuddering in Edith's presence once again.

Lou would have none of Edith's tricks. She asked why Edith came on as she did. After their first few meetings, Lou yawned and rubbed her pink eyes. Matter of factly, she said, "Hilda, you better get rid of her. She's a killer for sure. She does it with sugar, convinces you that you need her, see? Once you're in her trap, she's in control. If you don't dance to her tune, she moves in for the kill."

Hilda lay on the bed, remembering Lou's prophetic words, and she started to laugh. She became hysterical, her laughter going out of control, filling the room.

After Hilda got up, she puttered around the house and swept the webs from the ceiling again. As she dressed for work, she searched for the words that needed to be said to Edith. They filled her head and stood like large blocks of wood standing neatly in a row.

The spiders were gone. The house was clean and quiet. Hilda looked around the room and said aloud, "I'm leaving now." She hummed and went out the door.

Family
Photographs

Pawnee village (Nebraska) shortly before removal to Indian Territory (1811).
Courtesy of Smithsonian Institution, National Anthropological Archives

Captain Jim in Indian Territory.
Courtesy of Hilda and Wadsworth Howell

Last surviving Pawnee Scouts/Robert Taylor in headband (c. 1930).
Courtesy of Nebraska Historical Society

Lena Arkeketa (right) with younger sister Bertha (c. 1898).
Courtesy of Esther M. Childs Gooden

Lena Arkeketa (on left) with schoolmates.
Courtesy of Esther M. Childs Gooden

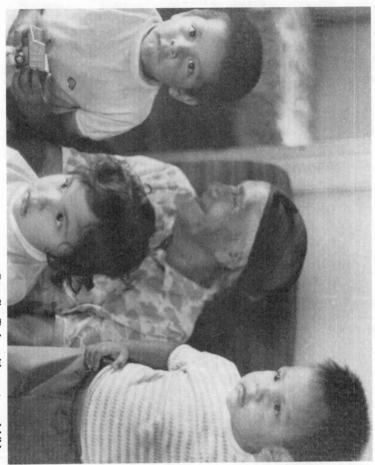

Cora Jim Taylor with great-grandchildren.
Courtesy of the author

Lena Hartico (née Arkeketa) with the author, her granddaughter (c. 1948).
Courtesy of Luther McGlaslin family

Author's mother (1955).

Author (in braids) with younger sister.
Courtesy of Juanita McGlaslin

Nakai Nez Bitsilly and Hoskon Tsosie's Daughter.
Courtesy of John Walters family

Indian
Time

Preface

My timepiece says it is "Indian time." The term is often used lightly by contemporary Indian people while non-Indians wonder about its meaning and are sometimes derisive. Indian time conveys an old grasp of time and life, perceived and experienced collectively by Indian people. It is a perception of themselves experiencing time in respective tribal societies. Time observed in this manner is not required to be exact. *Eight o'clock promptly on the dot* is an artificial time measurement, for time is not measured. Rather, its dimensions are noted. Life experience and the duration of a people are recorded in generations of offspring who carry on the perceptions. Time makes no promises to us nor guarantees anything. The phenomenon of time is not influenced by us, although we are poignantly affected by it. Continual, illusive, and intangible—it is unpredictable yet consistent.

We have need, therefore, to note a child's first laugh aloud, and this is recognized in ceremony. The coyote's season comes upon us, and stories of him are told only at that time. Birthing rituals and ceremonies of death, the distance from grandmother's final resting place to ours and our children's, shows just where we've been. This is the only way to count time, if indeed it can be counted.

I am an American Indian, but this simply does not say enough to satisfy the past, present, or future. I am a Pawnee. I am an Otoe. I am a woman and "companion" (the Navajo term for the spouse) to my husband. I have mothered children and dreams. I have heard the ancient stories, the beginnings of peoples and things. They are not finished yet. I find myself *here* and often look behind me to see the path where the people have been. From this place and essence, the sum of identities, an odyssey unfolds.

Indian people today (especially those of Plains origins) have often been told that all the "real Indians" are "gone," and that those who remain are somehow less than their predecessors and that we are locked safely away from the mainstream of society in time and cultural gaps we cannot escape. This is a heavy burden on the grandchildren of those real Indians who are gone. It is a weight on the spirit, and the time for it to be lifted has come.

We have read that those real Indians were once as a great and mighty mystical cloud that enveloped this continent. A century ago, more or less, the wind blew ominously (fanned by the hands of a "new" man, and time not Indian). The cloud broke up, drifting aimlessly for a while, and then dispersed into thin air. Where it went, only those real Indians know for sure. Just like that—they disappeared. An image comes to mind of vulnerable people easily affected by intrusions from beyond their worlds. The remnants of the fading people rise photogenically, but they are compelled to voluntarily drown themselves in the inevitable melting pot of cultures. In they go, one at a time, into the pot that simmers. So the story is told that those people, Indian, rode into a splendid sunset never to return, while the new man was the only witness to their exit.

Where is it that the real Indian has gone? And who are *we,* the grandchildren of those who are gone?

They said that his demise would be inevitable, his destruction was even perhaps justifiable, and eventually he would pass away into extinction anyway. This is what we were taught repeatedly. The message became loud and clear. With some apology, but very efficiently, as children we were instructed in this lesson throughout our contact with formal education. The words always went over our heads. The messenger hypnotically refused to see *us*. The words bounced on the past, the future, and around in our lives. We emerged, but often bruised and sore.

Dare we as children and adults ask where and why the real Indian has gone? Forever? Did he really disappear? Mysteriously? Romantically? Is he alive and well? Is he in hiding, marking life and experience by Indian time? Will he survive? Is there hope for him? Or did he exit resigned to his death? In tragedy? Majestically, or apathetically? Drunkenly? If he met his death, was it from a natural cause? Did he pass away peacefully in his dreams? Or was reality the source of death? Did he take his own life? Tell me, was he a victim of foul play?

When the real Indians succumbed a century ago, were their unborn grandchildren expected to yield their birthright also? Was the future laid to rest with the ancestors? Were Indians of two hundred years ago more Indian than those a century after them?

An appalling fact is that Native children in Indian America, from the time they enter school, are constantly exposed to these kinds of charges and implications.

We have all heard it said that on the surface the tree bends with the wind, but the roots go just as deep. Time does not discriminate. It is one of the realities touching all people, influencing all cultures. Change must occur. It is a fact of time, and the transformation of people is what this odyssey relates.

The Indian is often presented merely in reference to the past, and always it is a history told not by Native Americans. We find him poised in text or on screen, penned by an author or directed by one who is carefully aloof and removed from today and the people. It is preferable, though, to catch a surrealistic glimpse of the Native American today in the flesh where he stands on the horizon which separates Mother Earth and Father Sky. Yesteryear he was prodded there, pushed to the brink of extinction. But he had no intention of taking the plunge over the edge, or surrendering his identity, or sacrificing himself to a melting pot of conformity. He meant to endure and survive. In a precarious stance, he clung by a thin lifeline. Now he is on the horizon of tomorrow.

Time has passed. We mark it by hindsight, experience, the diminishing of one people and the flourishing of others. We find ourselves *here*.

This is an intimate look at an American Indian family that was nurtured on this line where the ancestors stood earlier, the horizon of the American Indian. Here on this plane some people yet cling tenaciously to threads of Indian time that stretch from the ancient beginnings through the present. From the edge of Indian time overlooking infinity, there is acute perception and perspective. We, a people, have been there and have seen the omens that warn of the abyss beyond.

Today there remains a compelling and understood (but often unspoken) obligation among Native people to survive as such. It is the same obligation the ancestors experienced. In due Indian time, we shall know how well we fared. In the meantime, miraculously, we find ourselves *here* to look behind us and see the footprints on the path where the people have been. We put our feet on the prints to satisfy our own curiosity and to pass Indian time. And we move on.

The Pawnees

The Pawnees, like other contemporary Indian people, were on this continent long before the European arrived at its shorelines.

It is acknowledged by the Pawnees themselves that they are an old people who undoubtedly have seen much more of time than they currently remember. For numerous seasons they were in journey, on the road to today, traveling vast lands as uninhibited as the peoples of the time, following buffalo herds and other plentiful game until these were depleted. With time, the Pawnees would be depleted too.

The origin of the Pawnees evades explanation. Their name has been interpreted in several ways. Usually, by other Plains Indians, the name Wolf People is applied to the Pawnees, and this is undoubtedly an ancient designation. They have been called Pawnee for about 350 years in historical documentation.

The Pawnees became aware of the newly arrived man about the fourteenth century. Often the Pawnees eluded the newcomer and he, being unfamiliar with the terrain, did not locate the settlements of the Pawnee Indians immediately. As expeditions entered the Great Plains and contacted or "discovered" groups of people, the expeditions recorded the people they met. The locations of the tribes were also recorded, but the documentation was inconsistent, and new names were constantly being given to the people and towns.

With the settling of North America by these new people, the Pawnees could not help but become increasingly visible. The territory which they and other groups had freely roamed for centuries was soon under newly raised flags. Later, all the land except for a few acres was inaccessible to the Pawnees.

There were four bands of Pawnee recognized in historic times by the U.S. government: the Chaui, the Kitkahaki, the Pitahauerat, and the Skidi. These bands are still distinguishable today. At various times these bands were referred to as the Grand Pawnee, the Pawnee Republic or Republican Pawnee, Noisy Pawnee or Tappage, and Wolf or Loup.

In 1818 each of the four bands made a formal agreement, or treaty, with the federal government. The contents of the agreements were identical.

At the time of the agreements the bands of Pawnee were living in an arrangement they had probably maintained for some time, at least a century. Their settlements or villages characteristically followed this plan.

Beginning in 1825, the four bands were officially recognized by the government as one tribe called Pawnee. The Treaty of 1825 placed the Pawnee Indians under the guidance of the United States. The Pawnees acknowledged the supremacy of the U.S. Regulation of trade was a provision. The laws of the U.S. were to ultimately rule, and the bands were not to supply arms to enemies of the U.S.

During this time, the Pawnees called much of Kansas and Nebraska home. Here they erected their mud lodges and villages. The mud lodges were extensions of the earth itself. It was in this environment, and to gain control of a portion of it, that other treaties were negotiated with the Pawnees.

In 1833, the Pawnees relinquished title to their hunting ground lying south of the Platte River, which would remain a hunting ground for use at "the pleasure of the President." It was also made accessible to other friendly Indians.

Compensation for the land to be paid in goods, was $4600 for twelve years annually, or a total of $55,200 in merchandise. The four bands were also to receive agricultural implements for five years. Schools were provided for in a $10,000 sum to be paid in full in ten years time, at $1,000 per year.

Blacksmiths were to be provided the tribe, as well as a farmer, oxen, and other necessities. The Pawnee Nation renewed its fidelity to the United States and pledged peace with neighboring tribes in the area.

As a result of the treaty, the Pawnees were to relocate themselves on agricultural districts for a year, where assistance would be available to them. Protection of government officials and employees could also be better secured on these districts. Thus, agriculture was promoted. Agriculture was not new to the Pawnees, but the confines of the lifestyle were. The U.S. government thrust upon them things they had not previously experienced.

Twenty-five guns were to be distributed in each Pawnee village. This was their sole protection from other tribes while confined to these districts. Receipt of goods furnished by this treaty was then acquired. Finally, the treaty became binding when ratified.

The interpreter who helped negotiate the Treaty of 1833 was a man called La Chapelle.

The Treaty of 1848 at Fort Childs ceded a sixty mile strip of land on the Platte River. Payment, two thousand dollars, was in goods and merchandise. Timber on the land was made available to the United States. Friendship and fidelity were again pledged, and disputes were to be settled by the President.

Next was the Treaty of 1857. It absorbed all remaining land held by the Pawnees, except for a small area where a reservation was to be established. Payment was to be made over a period of five years at forty thousand dollars annually. At the expiration, thirty thousand dollars per annum was to be a perpetual annuity to the Pawnees.

The U.S. was to establish manual labor schools for the benefit of the Pawnees, and the Pawnees promised to keep their children in attendance. If they did not, there was to be a deduction in their annuity equal to the tuition lost. The U.S. was to supply tools, farming utensils, and stock. Dwellings and a mill were to be erected. Pawnees were to be friendly and not make war, except in self-defense. Forts and occupation of military posts on Pawnee land was allowed by the Pawnees, but other occupation was forbidden. The U.S. was to also furnish teachers of stock management. Offenders of the U.S. laws were to be surrendered to the President. Provision for the half-breeds of the tribe is peculiar to this treaty. Article 11 acknowledged services by five Pawnees as guides for U.S. soldiers. Article 12, the last, had to do with claims against the Pawnees.

Within the provisions of this agreement, compensation was made to a missionary who had befriended the Pawnees. This compensation amounted to two thousand dollars for services and goods he had supplied to the Pawnees. He had vaccinated them against smallpox when it was decimating them and fed them during lean times.

This information is significant because at the beginning of the nineteenth century, the Pawnees were estimated to be at nearly ten thousand people. In 1832 the start of smallpox epidemics were brought by emigrants, and these spread among the people and killed three thousand. Bodies decayed on the open plains because entire villages were overcome. Cholera followed in 1849 with "twenty thousand settlers and sixty thousand head of stock" plowing directly through Pawnee villages. Another one thousand Pawnees died.

A little more than a century ago the Pawnees left the land along the Platte, tore themselves from it. This act was not entirely voluntary. The reasons outnumbered the Pawnees.

In Nebraska, the Pawnee villages were semipermanent earth lodges. There is archaeological evidence indicating that the Pawnees, or their direct ancestors, were in the area consistently for several generations.

The Pawnees were constantly in a state of war with their neighbors in all directions. Their adversaries included the Sioux, Cheyenne, and Arapaho. In fact these three tribes were the traditional enemies of the Pawnees.

Pawnee villages sat in the middle of territory roamed by these three tribes. The Cheyenne and Arapaho were allied with the Sioux. The combined tribes extended across the Missouri River, over the Black Hills, and throughout western Nebraska. The Cheyenne and Arapaho were small in numbers compared to the Sioux. There were between three and four thousand people. But the Sioux, all together, were guessed to be many times that number.

Both sides waged a vindictive war against the other side that was perpetual and carried from one generation to another. The oral and written histories of these groups confirm this statement.

There were attempts at peace between the tribes. A few could even be described as humorous. One such effort to promote peace between the Sioux and the Pawnees occurred in 1864.

A general on horseback presided over this appeal for peace, which incidentally came from neither the Sioux nor the Pawnees, but from the federal government. At the general's side was a bugler. There were four interpreters present, two for each side. The general saluted each tribe. The bugler gave some impressive bugle calls. It lent sobriety to the occasion. There were eighty Pawnees present who were scouts for the government. There were about four hundred Sioux. The general delivered his prepared speech.

He related to his "brothers" how his heart ached because his "red children" fought as they did. He would like to see peace prevail. All red children were equally his he said. There was enough for all: grass, water, land, and game. He reminded the tribes of kinship and brother-hood. Progress was not possible with war. The "Great Father" wanted to see his red children become numerous and prosperous. To attain these things, there had to be peace. He wanted a promise from both tribes to leave the other alone, and he suggested that the strip of land the tribes held in common should remain a neutral area. If the Pawnees and Sioux would do everything he asked, the Great Father would be satisfied. In turn, he would help them when they suffered by issuing rations to keep them from starving. Then he asked how the Pawnees and Sioux felt about this proposition.

The first speaker, on the Sioux side, replied that he would like to please the Great Father. He himself was quite willing to leave the Pawnees alone, since he personally felt they didn't amount to much anyway.

The Pawnees sat on horseback saying nothing in words, but a good deal was said on their faces. A Pawnee wearing a pair of army trousers approached the general. He said that in olden times the Pawnees owned all the land south of the Platte. Then smallpox came and changed conditions for the Pawnees. Now, after being relocated, the Pawnees were settled again to everyone's satisfaction, including the Pawnees'. They preferred peace, but that would depend on the Sioux. Gradually the meeting deteriorated with each successive speaker.

Another Sioux speaker replied that there was no reason that he could see to change things because the Sioux were getting along fine, without peace with the Pawnees. And he wondered why it was that the Great Father expected peace from his red children when he could not stop his white children from fighting. This was in reference to the Civil War.

The meeting continued until sundown. By then the Sioux speaker was using sign language for the benefit of the Pawnees. He called the Pawnees liars, signifying a forked tongue with two fingers.

The Pawnees were uneasy and began to confer with one another. They returned insults when the Sioux speaker gave way to anger, yelling at the Pawnees in his own tongue.

The government officials became alarmed and decided to separate the two tribes at the general's request. Eventually a river separated them. The Sioux continued to yell from across the river, however, and the Pawnees returned some screams of their own.

Most contact between the two tribes was deadly serious.

The last battle on the field between the Sioux and Pawnees occurred in 1873. This, too, is significant because, aside from the fact that the Pawnees were defeated, humiliated, and numerous Pawnees killed, it took place at a time when the Pawnees were under the protection of the government. This battle and its circumstances, coupled with the aftermath of disease, greatly affected the few remaining Pawnees. They were a broken people.

The Pawnee reservation in Nebraska was ceded in 1876, and the Pawnees were removed to Indian Territory. By 1900 at Indian Territory, after disease took its toll and old enemies their revenge, the century of transition cost the Pawnees about nine thousand of their own people. There were only about 650 Pawnees recorded at the turn of the century.

In the words of an old man, "somewhere along the Platte River, Nebraska," a Kitahaki woman gave birth to a son. He did not know the exact date. In the spelling of Pawnee Agency, the woman was called Stah-pe-tah-we-ee. The son she bore was later called Ah-roose-ah-too-tah-it. He became a man with several names, but was most commonly called Good Horse and Robert Taylor. Robert Taylor is how he is remembered today.

His mother had one sister, the only aunt known by him. Sak-low-ooh was his aunt's name. As said previously, they were members of the Kitkahaki band. Robert Taylor had brothers and a sister. Lah-le-lou-lah-chiks-se-wa-la and Sah-kah-pah-uh were his brothers' names (again, all the names recorded here are in the agency spelling). Cha-ka-us, one of his mother's names, was given to his sister.

Robert Taylor's maternal grandfather was called Ah-le-kah-loh-lou. His mother's mother was Cha-tah-kah-lou-kah-low-koo.

The father of Robert Taylor passed away when the child was very young. His father had two names known by the Pawnees. In the Pawnee tongue, Tay-sah-kah-loo-koo was one name. In translation it meant He Is Making Shoes, or Shoemaker. The other name of his father, in the spelling of the Pawnee Agency, was Is-sup. No translation for his name is recorded. By word of Robert Taylor's grandchildren, via the old man, his father was a Frenchman.

La Chapelle, the interpreter for the Treaty of 1833, was a Frenchman. La Chapelle may have been a Pawnee, at least in part.

According to the missionary identified in the Pawnee Treaty of 1857, La Chapelle was a half-blood. La Chapelle may have been half Pawnee or possibly Arikara, which is the same family. La Chapelle spoke at least three languages: Arikara, Pawnee, and French.

There was a La Chapelle among the Pawnees in 1835. He was simply identified as a Frenchman "living with two Kitahaki wives." The Pawnees could not pronounce the name La Chapelle. It was particularly noted that their version of La Chapelle was I-sha-pa. It is likely the wives of this man were sisters, as it was the practice then to marry sisters. Prior to this, La Chapelle may have lived with an Arikara woman and her people. Supposedly, during his stay with the Arikaras, La Chapelle was nearly lynched by whites in retaliation for whites who were killed by Arikaras.

We know that La Chapelle was the interpreter for the Pawnees, and that he was summoned when the famous treaty expedition came into Pawnee country in 1833.

On June 27, 1843, La Chapelle was killed. The attack came from the Sioux on the village of the Kitkahaki Pawnee. When it was over, several Pawnees were dead, including La Chapelle (assuming he is considered a Pawnee). If the information is accurate, La Chapelle had spent his last decade in residence among the Pawnees who were said to be his own people.

Robert Taylor had few memories of his father, or of living in the village of mud lodges which were constantly being burned in raids by enemy tribes in his first years. As a child he probably went naked as the boys were permitted to do until they were about the age of five or six. The first name he was called was probably Takah, meaning White. Takah was a common name given to all the boys until they took other names.

When Ah-roose-ah-too-tah-it took that name, meaning Good Horse, it would be difficult to say. Pawnee historians offer the explanation for the name. In earlier days, one measured his status in horses. A man was allowed to take horses in raids and warfare. This was the way of life, a common practice.

Good Horse possessed fine horses. After the acquisition in the usual manner, he sold them. In this way he acquired a name as well. Granted it is a story one has heard before from several families in almost every tribe. The difference is that Good Horse sold his horses to the U.S. Cavalry. This was the beginning of an important relationship he held with the government.

Ah-roose-ah-too-tah-it was a Pawnee Scout.

The Pawnee Scouts, infamous today for their participation with the U.S. Cavalry in the Indian Wars, assisted in subduing other Indian tribes, primarily their traditional enemies.

The Pawnee Scouts have been described in two ways. The more derogatory is "mercenary soldiers." On the other hand, their commanding officers saw the scouts as "wonderful fighters to whom no written history has yet done justice." Both descriptions are extreme. How did the Pawnees call them? With a certain irony, every one of those scouts who lived to old age answered to an intimate name spoken only by their children and grandchildren: Grandfather.

Among their own people, the Pawnee Scouts were held in high regard. That is, until very recently when a few young Pawnees, not being familiar with Pawnee history, have held the aggressive actions of the Scouts against that generation. But on the whole, the Pawnees have always honored and remembered the Scouts through the empty times when there was little else worth recollection or honor.

The Pawnees never declared war against the United States. It is an act for which they have been historically proud. It has been stated that the tribe considered itself an ally of the U.S., but many Pawnees might discredit that. The Pawnees suffered drastically at the hands of the federal government. From the beginning the relationship between the tribe and the government was born of necessity for the survival of the Pawnees, and not of love. But the Pawnees also suffered pre-Western history at the hands of old enemies who knew the vulnerable Pawnees well. No, the Pawnees had no true allies, Indian or otherwise.

Today the Pawnee speak of only one tribe with endearment, and they perform a tobacco ceremony regularly with them as a gesture of this affection and tie. The tribe is the Wichita, who are close relatives of the Pawnees.

It is told that these two tribes stumbled onto each other a long time ago on the open plains. Until then they were not aware of the other's existence. They discovered they spoke similar languages and could communicate. Both tribes were greatly mystified by this and wondered over the puzzle. Because of this unsolved mystery, they made a bond then and there, a promise that they would never go to battle against the other. The promise is still good. Annually, they renew it by giving and receiving tobacco. This pledge, however, does not indicate that they were allies at any time, merely that they never fought one another.

In light of the fact that the Pawnees have always stood alone, therefore, much of what has been attributed to the Pawnee Scouts is correct. The Pawnees of days gone-by lived and died daily by means of war. They were a warrior people. The Pawnee Scouts in their own words have said their acts were bold and their loyalty was to no man except the Pawnees. They did not at any time, even during old age, feel compelled to alter their deeds with gentle descriptions of their lives.

The Pawnee Scouts were paid, as were other scouts for the government (who were Sioux, Cheyenne, Crow, Navajo, Apache, etc.). An act of the Thirty-Ninth Congress, "An Act to Increase and Fix the Military Peace Establishment of the United States" authorized this payment. Approved July 28, 1866, Section 6 states, "And the President is hereby authorized to enlist and employ in the Territories and Indian country a force of Indians, not to exceed one thousand, to act as scouts, who shall receive the pay and allowance of cavalry soldiers and be discharged whenever the necessity for their further employment is abated, or at the discretion of the department commanders."

The Pawnee Scouts began their service in the fall of 1864 when a general came to recruit the Pawnees at the Nebraska reservation. He held a council with the chiefs, and eighty young men left with him in a coveted opportunity to live the life of a warrior again, however briefly. These eighty men were the first Pawnee Scouts. They furnished their own horses. The government was to provide arms and rations, and they were paid twenty dollars a month.

It was in October 1864 that Good Horse enlisted in Company A of the Pawnee Scouts. He was not mustered into service, however, but was rejected for impaired vision.

In 1864, the military was defending the Union Pacific Railroad against other Indians. The Power River campaign of 1865 followed. The Pawnee Scouts participated with one hundred Winnebago or

Omaha scouts. The Battle of Summit Springs near the Colorado and Nebraska border in 1869 involved Tall Bull of the Cheyennes and his Dog Soldiers. The service of the scouts was intermittent, spanned several years, and terminated in the spring of 1877.

In 1869, an Ah-roose-ah-toot-tah-it enlisted and was assigned to a detachment of Pawnee Scouts. He was thought to be about twenty years of age, but age often was guessed.

Years later in Indian Territory an elderly Robert Taylor made a declaration for a pension. He was the same person who had enlisted at the Pawnee Agency in Nebraska. During his enlistment, the scouts primarily guided the Union Pacific Railroad.

Documents from this time period give contradictory information regarding Robert Taylor's physical appearance. He is described at one time as being very light with brown eyes and hair. At another time he is said to be very dark with black hair and eyes. It all depended on who gave the description. Robert Taylor, talking about himself, added that his face was scarred from the smallpox which stalked the Pawnees in his youth.

A Skidi Pawnee added another recollection of Robert Taylor. He recalled that Robert Taylor was present, as he was, at the scouts' encampment near Pike's Peak while the Cheyennes, under Chief Tall Bull, were being pursued.

Robert Taylor said that in the year the Pawnees were massacred by the Sioux, he'd lost his discharge papers. Therefore, he was attempting to prove that he was a Pawnee Scout in order to receive a pension. The massacre in question occurred in 1872, according to Robert Taylor. But he may have meant 1873. The last confrontation at Massacre Canyon, Nebraska was in the summer of 1873. In August, the Sioux under Spotted Tail won a crushing victory over the Pawnees.

The official service of the Pawnee Scouts terminated in the spring of 1877, the year Red Cloud surrendered. They were there on October 24th and saw Red Cloud, their old and alarming enemy, a prisoner of the U.S. Cavalry. Forty-two Pawnee Scouts were involved in the incident, after riding a distance of a hundred miles to join forces with the cavalry at midnight, prior to the day of Red Cloud's surrender. The

Pawnees successfully removed all the horses from Red Cloud's camp without being discovered. Later, Red Cloud surrendered peacefully to the army. But in his old age and in his memoirs, Red Cloud greatly regretted this sour fate which had befallen him: the participation of the Pawnees, his avowed life-long adversaries, in his final capitulation.

The campaign from Crazy Woman Fork to Red Fork near Powder River, Wyoming in November located the camp of Dull Knife, the Cheyenne. Indian scouts were numerous in that campaign and included not only Cheyenne, but also Arapaho and Sioux, who were allies of the Cheyenne. Others were Shoshones, Bannock, Ute, Nez Perce, and Pawnees.

It was impressed upon all the scouts that any Indian scout who killed a child or woman would be dealt with severely. Although all Indian scouts were often accused of being merciless, it was also noted in military documentation that these scouts were frequently considered to be ineffective in battle. This complaint originated because it was generally agreed that the Indian scouts preferred to ride off in chase of prized horses rather than struggle with the opposition. For this reason, scouts were often reprimanded.

The highest number of Pawnee Scouts in the Pawnee battalion at a single time was two hundred men. In thirteen years of service, the Pawnee battalion lost only one man. He was of the Kitkahaki band.

Somewhat skeptical witnesses to those vanished times reported that a few of the Pawnee Scouts demonstrated strange and mysterious behavior when circumstances permitted. It was claimed that they were masters of illusion. One impressing feat which never failed to arouse wonder, and one which the Pawnees performed repeatedly, was that of seemingly altering one's physical appearance and transforming oneself into an animal, such as a deer. The magician would then dramatically appear as himself again. These demonstrations were honorable pastimes among the Pawnee, and were occasionally full-time occupations for a knowledgeable and skilled man or woman.

Captain Jim was such a man. He, too, was a Pawnee Scout, and a "doctor," which is a Pawnee description for a person involved in healing the mind or body.

Captain Jim, under the name Koot-tah-we-coots-tah-kah, enlisted in 1867 and served intermittently until 1877.

Koot-tah-we-coots-tah-kah meant White Hawk. He also used the name Sky Chief, Lah-roo-rah-ah-huks-sty-sah-lu. And it is probable that he used several other names as well.

It happened that during his enlistment there was another Pawnee Scout who also used the name Koot-tah-we-coots-tah-kah. In fact, there were six men who shared three names. It was amusing to the Pawnees at roll call to see the scrambling of two men for the same name. But it proved to be confusing as well. To simplify the identity crisis the men were dubbed First and Second.

For clarification, Captain Jim became Koot-tah-we-coots-tah-kah, First. He and Koot-tah-we-coots-tah-kah, Second, had an identical military history. Both were discharged in April of 1877.

Koot-tah-we-coots-tah-kah took the name Captain Jim either during or after military service. It might have been on one of the evenings after the Pawnee Scouts had engaged in battle, or the name may have simply been given to him with his uniform and arms. It is known that the Pawnee Scouts did perform a scalp dance after battle and adopted other names in the course of service.

At one point during his enlistment, Captain Jim's horse was shot from under him. When the horse dropped to the earth, its weight fell onto his left knee and slightly injured it. Immediately afterward, he hemorrhaged from the lungs. The incident left him with a slight limp for the rest of his life and often, after this, he spit out blood when coughing.

Captain Jim was born into the Pitahauerat band in Nebraska about 1836. His father was called Making Himself Chief, See-tee-de-tah-kee-tah-we-loo-coo. The father of Making Himself Chief was called Fox. Say-suh-pah-tos was the mother of Making Himself Chief. The translation for her name is now lost.

Making Things Good, Chay-too-lay-way-lee-coo, was Captain Jim's mother. And her mother was Stah-kee-tah-we-lah-lee-coo, or Making Herself A Queen. She was renowned as a doctor with an unsurpassed reputation still remembered today. Captain Jim was undoubtedly influenced by this woman, for he, too, was eventually sought as a healer of sorts.

The Pawnees embarked upon a new road which led to Indian Territory about the time of Captain Jim's termination from the military. Ways of viewing the world, and life, previously grasped and interpreted from the boundaries of the Platte and from atop dome-shaped mud lodges, were being disrupted and destroyed. The Pawnees tried to heave extensions of the Nebraska world into Indian Territory. Mud lodges were erected there, and the older people worked to ignore the radical changes in their social and natural environments. But they felt the gap between the two worlds immediately, attempting to bridge it as best they could.

All too soon, young Pawnee people, having never felt firsthand a warrior's thrill of glory, a medicine man's power, the special turf of sacred and ancient origins, would forget that older Pawnees once spoke of a Pawnee life that began before time as we know it.

But miraculously the Pawnees did survive as a people, in the physical and "legal" sense—the latter being extremely important to those individuals and tribes who wish to sustain a collective tribal identity within American society. The old Pawnee spirit was rekindled as well, broken though it may have been in Nebraska a century ago. The unborn children in Indian Territory would mend it.

While in Nebraska, the Pawnees had the custom of taking a number of wives. This custom was permissible in several tribes, and often it was necessary.

The Pawnee culture and lifestyle was based on the hunt and the mobility of the hunter. The women managed gardens and collected natural foods near the mud villages to supplement the main diet of meat. Twice a year the tribe went on major hunts: the summer and winter hunts in which they followed the buffalo and other game. These treks lasted several weeks as the kill was to supply the bulk of the food for quite some time. During the hunts the people lived in temporary dwellings.

Agriculture, of course, could be practiced in only the stationary settlements where gardens were tended regularly. Even then, farming was limited, taking into regard the safety of the women whose task it was. Plundering of villages and gardens, and occasionally the total destruction of both, was common when enemy tribes were marauding.

Therefore, a coordination of efforts was greatly desired by Pawnee men and women. Blending and sharing special tasks and roles was encouraged and rewarding for both sexes. In peacetime, male and female roles were durable but flexible. In wartime, there was no discrimination. All could be warriors given the opportunity—the women, the children, and the elderly inclusive.

Marriage, if it was sound, brought one status, prestige, and security, in addition to caring. Both parties gained a very real trust for their very lives.

Perhaps the ratio of men to women also influenced these kinds of marriages, where a man took for himself more than one woman and the added responsibility of each additional wife. In any case, some Pawnee men had more than one wife.

Captain Jim had seven wives. His first marriage was plural. His first wife was a woman named Skah-ta-kee. She died near Pawnee, in Indian Territory. She had a sister, and this sister was the second wife in the marriage, and she also died. His second marriage was to Stah-pee-dah-ee-kah, also called Stah-kah-dee-coos-tay. She died. In his third marriage, the fourth wife was called Jennie by the whites. Her name was pronounced Stee-rah-tee-oo-lee-lit. Jennie's sister was the fifth wife. Both died before his next marriage, which was to Hannah. The deaths of his earlier wives were all attributed to their low resistance to disease.

Hannah and Captain Jim were divorced. He was married once more, to a woman whose girlhood name was Stah-ee-wah-do-koo. While attending school in Nebraska the superintendent there gave her the name Fannie, but she quickly forgot the last name he gave her. She knew Captain Jim in Nebraska. He was older than she. They were married by a license, which was a new practice to the Pawnees in Indian Territory. She lived eight years with him and was his wife when he died in 1916. He was about eighty.

In Pawnee custom, Robert Taylor had three wives. Of his marriage he said, "My wives were sisters and I married them." The eldest was Cha-kah-ri-ku-sey-ri-ku. Her English name was Belle. Cha-key-rey-sa, or Sallie, was the second. Angie was the youngest one. Legally he took one wife. Under pressure from agency officials to marry only one woman at a time, he married the youngest by the new law. It was recorded in the county courthouse. He stayed with his three wives until their deaths. Belle died about 1919 from tuberculosis. Angie followed in 1921. Sallie died four years later.

The mother of these three daughters was Chac-tah-lee-cah-uh. Their father was E-coots-lah-lee-sah-loo. Translations are unavailable.

As the years passed in Oklahoma, the older Pawnees who were born in Nebraska passed away with them. While a handful of the scouts still remained, they were called upon from time to time to recount a life that disappeared before they did. As surely as the sun rose, they knew, too, that they must go the same way. With their leaving, an intimate link the Pawnees had with an illusive past in old familiar territory would be severed.

The frail men in 1910 were viewed quite differently in 1864. They were youthful and had been issued a regulation uniform at their enlistment: a pair of trousers, a blouse, and a hat. The hats they did not much care to use. If the hat fell beside the way, to the Pawnees it was no loss. Their horses actually wore the hats more often than the men did. The Pawnees cut holes in the top of the hats for their ponies' ears to stick through. And the blouses were often tied to their saddles rather than worn on their backs, which they preferred bare. Their trousers, sooner or later, had the seat cut out, and were separated into two sections held up by a belt. The seat was replaced by a breech cloth. From time to time the trouser legs would also come off, and the men would ride free as they had been taught.

Needless to say, the alterations the Pawnees made to their uniforms immensely frustrated the other enlisted men who accompanied them. It appears as if later in service, the scouts kept the entire uniforms as souvenirs, for they surfaced on special occasions in Indian Territory when the old scouts pulled them out of storage.

The Pawnees rode their own horses with Indian saddles and bridles most of the time. Beside the government carbines and knives, a few had lances, tomahawks, or bows and arrows. The scouts would also adorn their horses when possible. They generally kept their horse's hair braided because they found it useful to grip when mounting the horse, or especially helpful when a man needed to drop to the horse's side to escape bullets and arrows.

Fifty years later in Oklahoma the former Pawnee Scouts would bring out of storage those garments and adornments worn by themselves or their horses. The mementos and memories would gently stir and rouse the people. Especially on Veterans' Day the surviving scouts, fewer each year, would be honored by their tribesmen. The Pawnees would prepare a feast and a war dance on that day. The scouts would attend, supported by canes and relatives. The old men were then experiencing a new battle—growing old without sight and sound. But they would put on a cavalry coat (which still fit) and parade for the newer generations. The elderly men would don leggings, trimmed in fringe of human hair, and moccasins. When wearing this apparel, their hair was usually braided. But there was a former head chief and scout who is especially remembered because he continued to wear the scalp lock all through his days. In this style most of the head was kept bare, except for a strip of hair that hung from the top and back of the head.

Today the Veterans' Day memorial continues. It remembers Pawnee veterans of more recent wars (World War II, Vietnam, etc.), but there is an overwhelming presence of long-expired warriors that lingers with and in the people.

Robert Taylor died in 1930. He was about ninety, more or less. He had become totally blind and disabled, dependent on others for his simplest necessities. He was catered to, hand and foot, by his children and grandchildren who so fondly speak of him.

They said:

"He spoke Pawnee all the time and often made use of an interpreter. We grandchildren teased him affectionately, and he always returned the gesture. As he advanced in years, his eyes weakened and he did not see well. Often he

put his shoes on the wrong feet. Then he would notice his
mistake. He became impatient with himself for continuing
to make the same mistake. He had only one eye. The other
had been lost in an accident. He always wore a patch or
scarf over that eye. In those days, Pawnee children were
taught these manners: Never notice an obvious physical
handicap. Behave as though the handicap does not exist.
Do not draw unwanted or unsolicited attention to an in-
dividual with a physical loss or injury. This was one of the
few things for which a child might be punished (if he did not
heed the advice). To this day, everyone remembers that
Robert Taylor wore a patch over his eye, but we did not in-
quire as to how he lost his eye.''

Old man Taylor was photographed about three or four years prior
to his death, posing with the last survivors of the Pawnee Scouts.

Robert Taylor and his wives produced several children. His youngest son was by Angie. The child's name was Hugh Ralph Taylor. Taylor's life was brief, but he did have time to marry and father his own
children.

In 1920 he married a Pawnee woman called Cora Jim, after his
father advised him that he should.

Cora Jim's father was Captain Jim. Her mother, Jennie, was the
fourth wife of Captain Jim. Since her father was best known as Captain Jim, Jim became the family's surname. She was reared by the
Pawnee family of Julius Caesar after her mother's death. The head
of the family, Julius, was closely related to her mother.

When the Pawnees were first put under the supervision of a lo-
cal agency, there were several people (families and individuals) with
identical names, as explained earlier. To avoid confusion in paperwork,
and to simplify the dilemma of spelling names agency officials couldn't
even pronounce, these officials took it upon themselves to issue new
names which they could pronounce and spell. (Never mind that some
Pawnees would never do either with the names they were assigned.)
In a few rare cases the people picked names for themselves, however

most names were given at random. This is how and why there are some very conspicuous names among the Pawnees today.

Cora Jim went to school, unlike her parents. It was a newly erected boarding school located in the small community of Pawnee, Oklahoma. She spoke, read, and wrote fluent English. She also spoke Pawnee fluently, since it was her first language.

She had been married previously and had five children before Robert Taylor initiated her second marriage. She was eleven years older than her new husband. She had two daughters by the second union and was carrying her third child when her young husband died from tuberculosis. Not long after, she bore a son who was given his father's name.

The daughters of Cora Jim would mark time by the children they nourished. The older would marry a man of her own tribe, a member of the Skidi band. The younger would marry out of the tribe and into another. Together the two women have reared and mothered numerous children.

It is said among several Indian peoples that the first to bring life, to bear fruit, was The Earth. For this reason, she is bestowed with the appropriate name—that of mother.

I consider both of the daughters of Cora Jim to be my mother. But the youngest bore me. Grandmother was a Pawnee. Her mother was a Pawnee, and her mother's mother was also. And the mother of that woman was a Pawnee too.

I have often asked myself, when I am alone, if it is not possible that the very first mother (The Earth) is not Pawnee as well.

The Otoes

It has been written that the Otoe-Missouria Tribe was small a hundred years ago, and even three centuries before that. Technically, the Otoe-Missouria Tribe, as it is called today, was originally two tribes: the combined tribes of the Otoes and Missourias. They numbered approximately 450 people, including the Missouria, who by themselves were less than one hundred people when they joined, or more correctly, rejoined, their close kin, the Otoes. This occurred about 1800 when the Missouria Tribe was on the verge of extinction.

It is also claimed that the Otoes and the Missourias, with the kindred Iowa Indians, are from the family of Winnebago Indians. At some time, and for vague discrepant reasons, small groups broke away from larger ones to migrate southward from the area surrounding the Great Lakes.

The oral history is, as evidence seems to support, that a large common group migrated into what is now Iowa and remained there for a few years. A segment of the people, now called the Iowa, elected to stay. The Otoes and Missouria people continued their journey southward together until the Missourias found their way to the mouth of the Missouria River. At the turn of the eighteenth century, the Otoes were distinguished from the Iowa and Missouria and were pinpointed between the two groups in or near the present state of Iowa. A century later, however, the Missourias had chosen to reunite with the Otoes, and the two, then identified as one group, were in Nebraska and part of Kansas.

Ne-br-ra-tha-ka was once the Otoe world where they made villages and dwellings of earth, bark, and skin lodges along the Platte and Missouri Rivers.

In 1804 the Otoes were visited by Lewis and Clark. Lewis wrote of the Otoes and their perspective on the country they inhabited, "They have no idea of the exclusive possession of any country, nor do they assign themselves any limit. . . ." On the heels of Lewis and Clark's departure came the settlers.

The Otoes and Missourias made their first treaty with the United States in 1817. Among the dozen Otoe men who signed this treaty was Chongatonga, or Big Horse. The Treaty of 1825 provided for the regulation of trade through the Otoe country. One of the men signing the treaty was Shunk-co-pe or Choncape, who was said to be a descendent of Big Horse of the 1817 treaty. His name was translated to mean Big Kansas, and with a delegation of Otoe, Kansa, Omaha, and Pawnee representatives, he visited President Monroe at the White House prior to the 1825 treaty. There he had his portrait painted. It remains hanging in the White House today.

After the territory west of the Mississippi was opened in 1830, the Otoes, with several other tribes, ceded their common hunting grounds to the U.S. At this time they also ceded land which was exclusively theirs for a future reservation for the half-breeds of the combined tribes: the Nemaha Half-Breed Reservation. It is possible that Choncape, using another name, also signed this agreement.

Three years later the Otoes agreed to "abandon the chase for the agricultural life." In 1836 they agreed that lands which they had ceded would become part of the state of Missouri. The Otoes' portion of the payment for this part of Missouri was to be $1,050 in merchandise for the lands they relinquished with the Yankton and Santee bands of Sioux and Omaha. The Missourias received $1,000 in merchandise.

The Treaty of 1854 ceded all the Otoe country west of the Missouri River, except for a strip of land along the Big Blue River. The Otoes agreed to vacate the ceded lands and relocate on a strip which amounted to an area ten miles in width and twenty-five miles long. The treaty was signed by five Otoes and two Missourias. The first Otoe to sign was a man called Ark-ke-ke-tah, or Stay By It. He was a son of Choncape.

Arkeketa meant to Stand And Wait, or Wait On Each Other, but it was interpreted in a variety of ways, such as Stands-By-It, Watchman, Stay-By-It, Stands And Waits On It, and Herder.

Arkeketa, born sometime between 1812 and 1815 was the original Chief Arkeketa. Later his descendants would claim this same title, but written histories often confuse these men.

In 1837 the grandson of the late President Harrison wrote a letter to then President Van Buren on behalf of "Atteketa, War Chief of the Otoes," in which Arkeketa was represented as a friendly chief who assisted travelers when they passed through Otoe country. Arkeketa, with six of his principle men, desired to obtain for themselves the medals which the federal government was then conferring on prominent chiefs who visited the "Great Father." He also desired "a big paper" to state that he was a friend of the government. He thought he might carry this paper on his person and enhance himself among the incoming settlers and government officials.

Whether Arkeketa secured the medals he desired is not known for certain, but it is quite probable. Later, within the Arkeketa family, there were numerous medals that had been procured by several members of the family.

The big paper requested by him in a 1837 letter may have initiated other correspondence among government officials concerning the status of Arkeketa. There was definitely correspondence concerning him, but not all of it was favorable. In a document penned twenty years later, however, "Ar-ka-ke-tha" was again identified as a chief who had chastised members of his own tribe, as well as other tribes, for molesting emigrants passing through Otoe land. For securing and returning stolen goods to these emigrants, Arkeketa gained notoriety.

In 1854 Arkeketa was named head chief and held the position for nearly a quarter of a century. To the Otoes, Chief Arkeketa was also known as Choe-doe-nah-ye, or Standing Buffalo, which was a clan name. (He was a member of the Buffalo Clan.) It is very odd that on most documents concerning Chief Arkeketa, there is no reference to this name. When old Chief Arkeketa abdicated, it was to a son who was born in 1843. Both these chiefs, and another Arkeketa, were acting in the capacity of chief during the trying period of Otoe removal from Nebraska to Indian Territory.

The Otoe, from the time of Lewis and Clark to their removal to Indian Territory in 1881, experienced drastic change and turmoil. Much of this originated from the fact that the tribe did indeed occupy choice land greatly coveted by the settlers. Chief Arkeketa himself appealed to the government for help in the fall of 1854 in stopping the advancement of whites on the villages. During this period, formal education was also introduced, as was reservation life. A mission school was started in 1833, but the Otoe-Missouria burned it eight years later. Getting the tribe onto a small reservation required several years just to persuade them that such an act was in their best interest. To add to the tribe's difficulties in this era, the tribal agents appointed to them were often corrupt, or religious fanatics, and on occasion they had no agent acting on behalf of them at all.

A supplemental treaty was signed on December 9, 1854. It provided that the tentative reservation be moved five miles to the east side of the Big Blue River. The tribe felt this area offered a more defensible location and provided timber to them as well. They began their move onto their first reservation of 162,000 acres in Nebraska shortly thereafter, but not before squatters were already on the newly ceded lands prior to their being open to settlement.

For twenty-six years, about five hundred Otoe-Missouria people lived on the Big Blue Reservation. Again, the government attempted to make farmers out of them. Christianity was also imposed upon the tribe. Persistent pressure was applied to the people subjugating them to adapt to the whiteman's lifestyle. Internal strife and conflict began as tribal members tried to decide how to respond to the indignities they suffered.

About this time, one of the Otoe agents took thirteen thousand dollars of the Otoe annuity and left the reservation. The tribe, including women and children, gave chase. Though they finally managed to get a portion of the annuity returned, the Office of Indian Affairs soon dropped the controversial matter.

The difficulties with the agents persisted, and Arkeketa often defied them. One of the agents then created an Indian police force to bring the tribe under his dominion, but Arkeketa was another matter. The agent solved his dilemma by simply appointing a new head chief in 1863, undermining the tribe's social and political network that had existed and worked effectively to date.

The Big Blue Reservation had always been sought by the settlers, and from the time the tribe relocated there, speculation ran high that the reservation would also be available for settlement in the near future. The Otoes' new agent was himself in favor of opening it up to the settlers. The Otoe-Missouria census was at 465 persons, and the Superintendent of Indian Affairs suggested that the Big Blue Reservation could easily support 15,000 people. Allotments for the Otoes were then recommended, though the Otoes bitterly resisted the idea. Despite tribal protest, a survey of the reservation was requested by officials.

The period from 1867 to 1869 was extremely harsh for the tribe, who had to contend with reduced rations, severe winters, and an alarming mortality rate.

Another treaty was negotiated in 1869 when an Otoe delegation visited Washington, but the treaty was never ratified. It provided that a portion of the Big Blue Reservation, ninety-two thousand acres, be surveyed and appraised. Right-of-way for railroad lines on the west side of the reservation was secured at $1.25 an acre. According to the treaty, an Otoe-Missouria group would go to Indian Territory to explore land for new tribal settlement there, but the tribe could stay on the Nebraska reservation allotments if they opted.

One of the reasons the treaty was not ratified was that the Otoe-

Missouria agent strongly opposed removal. He felt that an allotment system was the answer for the Otoe-Missouria. He encouraged a complete kinship and cultural breakdown through the destruction of a village system. If this were to occur, he was sure that the Otoe-Missouria would then settle down and become Christian farmers. Another reason that the treaty was not ratified was the mixed reaction within the tribe itself. Part of the people considered removal a better alternative to staying on the Big Blue, especially with the close proximity of the whites on and near the reservation. Others felt that the tribe should cling to the land regardless of the hardships. The rift would eventually widen and split the tiny tribe.

Eight chiefs and one hundred other Otoe men petitioned the government, objecting to the provisions of the 1869 Treaty. This was submitted to the necessary offices. A newer plan was then proposed by the Otoes, that of selling the entire reservation rather than breaking up the tribe onto allotments. This new plan was ceremoniously applauded and encouraged by the Nebraska legislature.

Following this proposition, a delegation of tribal members left for Indian Territory. The purpose of the visit was to examine land which might be acceptable as the tribe's future home. The delegation would later return to the tribe and give their report on that part of Indian Territory they found desirable.

At this stage, tribal unity was undergoing tremendous strain. Emotions were intense. Nebraska had been admitted to the Union in March 1867, and hostile encounters occurred daily with the citizens of Nebraska. There were strong feelings in the tribe against abandoning territory that they had occupied for at least a century. Further tension had been instigated by the federal government which deliberately appointed men to the chieftainship who were sympathetic to the government and who would have otherwise not been in line for chieftainship at all. Sometimes the tribe supported those chiefs, and at other times did not recognize them and held them in contempt. As various chiefs fell out of favor with the government, more compromising men were officially recognized. Historically, chieftainship was hereditary through clans. There was a chief of each clan, and the number of clans determined the overall number of acting chiefs. Government selected headmen who were not recognized by the tribe. All these factors added to the Otoe-Missouria turmoil. But the predominant issue was that the tribe could not understand the reasons for their complete banishment from Nebraska in the first place. The antagonism and hostility within the tribe over rights to the chieftainship and the authority of traditional chiefs weakened it even more.

Two factions in the tribe began to surface. The most adamant group was in favor of moving away from the whiteman's presence in Nebraska. They came to be called the Wild Party or Wild Faction, principally by the agent who did not encourage removal to Indian Territory. Because of his counsel, he was extremely unpopular with the wild faction, who explained quite vehemently at every opportunity that they wished for the tribe to get as far away from the whiteman as possible and the civilization he carried with him. The Wild Party was also called the Coyote Band among the tribal members. The other faction sided with the agent, to a certain extent, on removal. The agent happened to be a Quaker and because his followers echoed his sentiments, they were called the Quaker Band. Most of that band were also members of the Society of Friends. In each band there were about 150 members, but there were uncommitted families who wandered back and forth between the two. The Quakers and the Coyotes were at constant odds, even though essentially they fought for the same thing—survival of the Otoe-Missouria people.

An 1872 act formally initiated the survey and appraisal of eighty thousand acres west of the Big Blue River. The issue of selling a part or all of the reservation was still a long way from being settled though. In 1873, five men representing the Otoe-Missouria Tribe visited the Commissioner of Indian Affairs in Washington to discuss this matter. One of these men was Arkeketa.

Actually there were two meetings held. The first was brief and cordial, merely a greeting between parties. When the group met for a second time, tempers were short. The important point, of course, was the selling of the Nebraska reservation, but an upcoming buffalo hunt was also discussed. The Otoe crop had been destroyed, and they had no food to subsist on in the winter.

The Commissioner reminded the Otoes that they had previously arranged and agreed to sell half their reservation, and he told them in no uncertain terms that it would be sold if anyone was willing to purchase it. The delegation knew very well that there were indeed buyers for it, though they did not state this. The Commissioner revealed that a change was about to overtake them, as he stated, "We white people are going to try to teach you how to live." The Commissioner wanted to extract an agreement from them, but the five men declined and continued to argue for the tribe's interest, reminding the official that they could not conclude business themselves. The final say depended on the people at home.

The Commissioner warned them that Congress had already passed a law allowing the sale of a portion of their reservation. At one point he declared that the Otoe-Missouria were behaving "foolishly" for having expressed doubt about selling a part of their reservation, having as much land as they did.

Chief Arkeketa declared to the Commissioner, "If you have a piece of land and I sell it, you would not like it."

The Commissioner replied that there was vast difference. The Otoe-Missouria were "children" of the government, and the government must take care of them. From time to time, children must be chastised by a responsible father. In some cases, children would be punished for misbehaving.

Medicine Horse, the most vocal of the Otoe delegation, bluntly suggested to the Commissioner that "There is such a thing as beating a child to death."

Throughout the entire meeting, Chief Arkeketa steered the conversation. Never letting the meeting falter, he directed it through to the end. The Commissioner, noting his presence and his name, acknowledged that "You are rightly named Stand-By."

As far as the Otoe-Missouria were concerned, the meetings in Washington settled little except that half the reservation would be sold.

A portion of the Coyote Band challenged the agent almost a year later by hunting buffalo on the Arkansas River without his permission. He had a few of the group returned. Medicine Horse was then emerging as the leader of the Coyote Band, along with Little Pipe. Medicine Horse eventually refused to live in the same village with the Quaker Band and set up his own village. Not long after, the agent had Medicine Horse's chieftainship stripped from him.

The Senate passed an act to survey and appraise 120,000 acres of the Otoe-Missouria Reservation in 1876. The land would be open to settlement for $2.50 an acre, and settlers would be able to purchase no more than 160 acres. However, to the outrage of the tribe, it was soon discovered that the entire reservation was being surveyed in 40-acre tracts. Even the Quaker Band was infuriated.

The Otoes, who Lewis earlier described as not having any "idea of the exclusive possession of any country. . . ," nor having previously assigned themselves ". . .any limit," now had a land base of forty-two thousand acres. They would not hold even that reduced amount for long. By 1877, the Quaker headmen were resigned to going to Indian Territory. The next issue to be resolved was when the tribe might move. Members of the Coyote Band, led by Little Pipe, were impatient and angered by squatters on the reservation. Refusing to make any more concessions, they left for Indian Territory in August 1877. The Quaker Band would stay in Nebraska until sale of the remaining land had been negotiated.

Little Pipe returned a few months later to lead more families to Indian Territory. The Indian police overtook them and escorted them back to the reservation. But other families successfully made their way to the Sac and Fox Agency in Indian Territory where the Coyote Band had been allowed to settle temporarily. Finally, the majority of the band, again under Little Pipe, made a bold escape. The Otoe agent called upon the Army to pursue Little Pipe, but the small group arrived in Indian Territory in late June.

The remaining reservation was sold in accordance with the Act of March 3, 1881. A delegation then visited Indian Territory to select a site near the Pawnee and Ponca Tribes already located there. With approval from the Secretary of Interior, the site was purchased with the Otoe-Missouria trust fund provided from the land sale of 1876. The entire tribe of Otoes and Missourias, scattered in remnants throughout Indian Territory, Nebraska, and Kansas, voted to accept the Act of 1881 and finally planned for a new home in Indian Territory.

The Otoe land in Indian Territory came to be in the area of Red Rock Creek. It amounted to a little more than 129,000 acres and it was the future. Prior to the Otoe acquisition, it had been set aside for the Cherokees as part of the Cherokee Strip. It was some forty miles away from the Coyote Band, which by then was being called the Absentee Band.

When the remainder of the tribe started for Indian Territory, they were on foot. The group was made up mostly of the Quaker Band, but others were also present. There were about 309 people, and they were accompanied by 11 white people, most of whom eventually married into the tribe.

The tribe's cattle herd, which they had begun in 1875, preceded the group by ten days. Tribal possessions were transported by wagons and ponies. The group left Ne-br-ra-tha-ka on October 5, 1881. It took them eighteen days to journey into Indian Territory. But arrive they did, somewhat pensive, disillusioned, and tired. Since October 23, 1881, the tribe has resided on Red Rock Creek which is still the center of Otoe-Missouria activity. The tribe includes ancestors of the members of the Coyote Band, most of whom rejoined the tribe by 1890. But a few were absorbed into the Sac and Fox Tribe who gave refuge to the Coyote Band earlier. Not all the tribal members who could have accompanied the group went to Indian Territory. Several families, all mixed-bloods, elected to stay in Nebraska on small farming tracts.

Among the Otoe-Missouria group who made the trek from the reservation in Nebraska were several children. One was a boy about eight years of age. His father was simply called Har-ti-coo, which in Otoe means Go Back. The boy's mother was a woman whose English name was Lizzie Rich.

Near Red Rock Creek, half a century later, an old man would relate to his children his account of that particular walk from Nebraska to Indian Territory. The child grew into an old man in Oklahoma, and he married twice. His name was Tom Hartico. His second wife was a chief's daughter. This woman had three names. Esch-ton-waw-she-gay-me, meaning First Born, was her clan name. Lena was her English name. Arkeketa was her maiden name, her Otoe family name.

Lena Arkeketa was born in 1884. Her father, George Arkeketa, was head chief of the Otoe-Missouria tribe between 1881 and 1896, the time of removal. According to a letter dated September 26, 1888, the Otoe agent again designated him chief. This chieftainship he shared with another man identified as John Joe. Additional documents dated in 1896 give George Arkeketa the head chieftainship as well.

He is also found on written documents under the name of Thin-chay-bus-kay, meaning Fluffy Tail, or Bushy Tail, which was a clan name. Another name recognized primarily by his family was Aw-tha-hun-ya, Crying Over Him.

He married an Otoe woman of French blood. Her clan name was Hroo-taw-daw-me. Her English name was Mary Diamond. She was born in 1856. Mary Diamond's father was called Wa-ta-co-ca. Translation is unavailable. Mary Diamond's mother was O-tar-tome. She was born about 1828 and was still living in 1900.

In his day, George Arkeketa was considered a radical for not conforming to government wishes on tribal and federal relationships. He often sided with the Coyote Band in Nebraska, and his sentiments were usually with tradition as opposed to breaking up the tribe in any manner or by any means. Several times he acted with the Coyote members or on their behalf. His strong opinions concerning the survival of the Otoe people got him into trouble, and it is generally agreed that he did not yield easily, nor was he humble. Described as a troublemaker in the language of the day, he was arrested more than once for leaving the Nebraska reservation without securing approval or a pass from whomever it was that held such authority. Besides being obstinate, he was sometimes guilty of being unreasonable. At times he took matters into his own hands. Land ownership, for instance, was a topic that absorbed him entirely, and he fought vigorously for Otoe interests in land matters. He visited Washington many times and on one occasion met the President. He received the usual medallions as tokens of his status. Undoubtedly the medals were always paid for by each tribe, in one way or another. Seldom were they simply gifts.

Nearly twenty years after bringing the tribe into Indian Territory, George Arkeketa died in January, 1901.

At that time, the Otoes lived in tents for the most part. They had not yet broken an old habit of moving about, and they favored mobility. Their agency locale had become a thriving community and even boasted a school. The Otoes also operated a ferryboat which added to their tribal income. Red Rock Creek was unpredictable. It rose to overflowing and then fell to the bottom depending on the rains. It was not unusual for people to attempt crossing at their own risk rather than paying the fee the Otoes charged. The Otoes would then recover goods and other possessions from the timber along the creek, and occasionally bodies as well.

George Arkeketa lived with his wife and children in a tent near the winding creek. He was ill with pneumonia. Although the Otoes had been issued allotments of land for cultivation, George Arkeketa had resisted these in Nebraska and was nearly the last holdout on allotments in Oklahoma. The government still expected the Otoes to change old habits and become farmers now that they were in Indian Territory. Receipt of an allotment was supposed to insure this transformation. George Arkeketa knew better. After much discussion, protest, and demonstration on his part concerning the Allotment Act, George Arkeketa finally gave up. Eventually he would be interred on his wife's allotment. It is said that he wished to be buried "on his own ground so that his grandchildren might walk on his grave," an Otoe expression.

He was put to rest in the traditional sitting position of the Otoes, overlooking a valley that would one day be passed to his grandchildren. He would be accessible there to his descendants.

George Arkeketa and Mary Diamond had two daughters and four sons. The daughters of prominent Otoe families and chiefs' daughters were entitled to some distinguishing marks of their own. Besides acquiring material goods, a young woman was often tattooed. Lena and her younger sister were tattooed on the center of the forehead as an indication of their status. Lena was a teenager then. Her parents, realizing the change the tribe would face, sent her to school, the same school erected at the agency her father had helped to establish. She would learn to read and write and do the usual things stressed at boarding schools in those days.

After she attended that school, she went to another some distance north from the tribal agency. It was a long ride, and the girls were young and told time not by the clock. Usually the day grew old before all the students were assembled and prepared to leave for the school. Then the wagon started down the road. Once, on one of these journeys, sometime after the girls had eaten the simple lunches they prepared for themselves, they became very drowsy. One girl, who was sitting toward the back of the wagon, fell off and was not discovered missing for some time.

Lena attended school until she was sixteen. Not much later she married, though her father discouraged it. Lena was very young, and her husband was older. Because her parents did not approve of this match, Lena met her future groom daily by the creek, away from her father's frown. Lena was often chaperoned by her younger sister, Bertha. Lena married Harry Childs and bore him five living children. During this marriage, she also gave birth to triplets, but they died immediately after they were born. Harry Childs is remembered today mainly for his involvement in the creation of the Church of the First Born, which used Peyote as a sacrament. The Church of the First Born existed only among the Otoe-Missouria Tribe and is not to be confused with the Native American Church which flourishes among several tribes today.

Within the Otoe-Missouria Tribe were people the tribe had taken in through adoption. One such man was called Gray Stone. Many years before the Otoe-Missouria were removed from Nebraska, a group of Otoe warriors came upon a massacre that had happened only minutes before. The victims were a small band from another tribe which the Otoes could not immediately identify. The people lay on the plains, and the Otoes dismounted from their horses and checked the victims to see if there were any survivors. The unfortunate ones included women, and when the Otoes rolled the people over to have a look at them, the Otoes were amazed to discover that one woman had a child in her arms. The woman had lived long enough to bring her baby to her breast to allow it to nurse, for it was untouched and unharmed. The Otoes picked up the baby and took it back to the tribe where it was given to a nursing woman and adopted by one of the Otoe men. The child enjoyed every right as an Otoe, though the people knew his background, and in their own way respected him as an Otoe and as someone who was a little different from them. Not long after the baby was rescued, the tribe sent out information to other tribes, letting it be known that they had discovered a baby and it was well and among them. Soon a Comanche group visited the Otoe. In the course of the visiting, it was agreed that the people who had been destroyed were Comanches. They insisted that the baby be kept among the Otoes, however, where it was being well taken care of. The baby grew up into a man called Gray Stone, and as an infant, a few days old perhaps, he became Otoe. Gray Stone married into the tribe and had three sons.

Lena's second match was to a son of Gray Stone's, but the two were not together for very long. She had a son with him, and then Lena was left to raise her six children alone.

For a while after that, Lena took to following her mother around. Her mother, Mary Diamond, had remarried and was constantly encouraging Lena to marry again also. But Lena was in no hurry, and besides there was no one to whom she was attracted, except one man. He was older than she, and he always seemed to be close by when Lena needed help. His name was Tom Hartico, the same man who made the walk from Nebraska to Indian Territory as a child.

Lena's children noticed that he was invariably near their tent at tribal doings and ceremonies. Then one of Lena's daughters observed that he seemed to visit Lena's mother often, talking very earnestly with her. Mary Diamond called on Lena and told her daughter that she would better off if she would marry again. Lena laughed and asked her mother, "Who would I marry?" Mary looked around and sighed and began to talk about Tom Hartico. Tom visited Lena afterward and looked expectantly at her, but she never gave any indication that she wanted to marry him. He didn't give up, though. He continued to stay around and visit often. One day he put Lena, with all her children, into his wagon, whipped his horses, and drove the whole gang to a nearby town where he and Lena took out a marriage license. Lena lived with him in a fine large wooden house on his allotment of land, where he kept numerous dogs. In time she bore him a son and a daughter. He died in 1952.

Lena Arkeketa died in 1967, but four of her children live on, not too far from the valley where George Arkeketa was put to rest. And his grandchildren played beneath his resting place watching the earth over him wear down. Tiny blue beads rolled to their feet from his resting place as they played.

Now Lena's children have children of their own, and I am one of them. My father was born of Lena's second marriage to Gray Stone's son, and I was reared in Grandpa Tom's big old house by him and Grandma Lena. They are gone now, but my father and many aunts and uncles are still here. And then, too, there are my children and grandchildren.

The Navajos

When the Navajos arrived in the Southwest is a date not fully agreed upon by scholars and anthropologists. There is speculation that they may have migrated here as early as 1000 A.D., but the sixteenth century is usually cited as a more acceptable date. Among the Navajos there is less confusion as to the journeys the people have made in their account of time and experience.

The first reference to the Navajos was made in 1583 by a Spanish expedition. Differentiation, though, between Navajos and Apaches, who are linguistically related, was not distinct until after 1626, and until then Navajos were frequently taken for Apaches. As Spanish expeditions entered the American Southwest, they encountered several Native peoples, but the seminomadic Navajos somehow managed to escape the fate of other tribes who were more accessible. They remained remote and aloof, at least temporarily. With the colonization of New Mexico, however, conflict and confrontation between the Navajos and New Mexicans was inevitable.

At the time of contact the Navajos were a large mass of people who affiliated themselves with various leaders, and the bands migrated from area to area, always in search of edible seeds and game. Groups of people wandered far and wide into present-day Arizona, New Mexico, Colorado, and Utah. The country they roamed was vast and rugged, encompassing deserts, canyons, mountains, and high plateaus that spanned millions of acres.

When the Spanish expeditions arrived in New Mexico, the Navajos dwelt in two main areas. The predominant one was a region of northwest New Mexico, now near the Colorado line, called Dinétah. It is the earliest area occupied by the Navajo as they are known today. The second area which had accumulated groups of people was Canyon De Chelly, or Tseyi. By 1700, the Dinétah area had been abandoned, probably due to warfare, and the people had moved westward where they are presently situated. Although Dinétah and Canyon De Chelly had large populations at particular times, there were hundreds of other Navajo people who lived in any number of places in addition to these two.

Dinétah, which means Gathering Place Of The People, is singularly important in Navajo oral history because it is the place in which many stories of Navajo origin are centered. Indeed, it is the place where the people evolved into the cultural group they are today.

The history of the Navajo includes warfare and raids. Even during the Dinétah occupations, where the people constructed crude fortresses, the Navajos were being harassed by the Utes from the north, the Comanches from the east, and the Spaniards with Puebloan allies from the south and east. In addition, there is evidence to support the fact that other Plains groups may have also ventured into the Dinétah region.

In Dinétah, the people became powerful and cohesive. They were made up of several groups with different origins, but the period is identified by the Puebloan people living with them.

By the time of the Pueblo Revolt of 1680, the Navajos had frequent contact with the New Mexicans. They often raided Spanish settlements, took livestock whenever possible, and captives as well. Both the Navajos and the Mexicans practiced slavery, with the New Mexicans carrying Navajo slaves as far as Sonora and Mexico City to be sold there or to be distributed among various households.

With the Navajos it was custom to adopt very young captive children as their own. Boys would grow up with all rights of the Navajo man. Girls, however, might be denied some rights given exclusively to Navajo women. In the seventeenth century, a few of these Spanish children rose to prominent positions among the Navajos.

For a period lasting about 150 years, from after the Pueblo Revolt of 1680 to 1846, the Navajos continued their raids against the New Mexicans, as the latter did against the Navajos.

In 1846 the American flag was raised over Santa Fe, ushering in a new period. Like the previous Spanish and Mexican governments, it was anxious to restore captives and property to the New Mexicans. The Americans intervened in the centuries-old dispute. Subsequently, for the insults received, the New Mexicans were told by the Americans to "retaliate and make war on the Navajos."

Only two treaties with the Navajos were ever ratified by Congress. One was signed in November 1846. Since it made no significant change in conditions between the New Mexicans and the Navajos, another followed a year later. It was never ratified.

The period between 1847 and 1849 saw warfare increase. By mid-1849, the Americans and New Mexicans were planning an extensive military campaign against the Navajos to annihilate them.

Also about this time, a military post called Fort Defiance was erected in an attempt to curb the expeditions into Navajo country by the New Mexicans. The Navajos protested its site, but eventually the Fort was completed. Later the Navajos burned it down. To add to this, raids by the Ute and Apache Tribes on the Navajos increased. This led to treaty negotiations with all three tribes. The idea of twenty- to forty-acre tracts to be assigned to each head of household was introduced. Such a plan would establish limits to Navajo country.

A gathering of some two thousand Navajos resulted. The New Mexican governor stipulated the boundaries of the Navajo land to the assembled group, explaining that a dividing line would promote peace. The Navajos were offered about seven thousand square acres. The governor later admitted that most of it was useless for cultivation.

Manuelito emerged as the spokesperson for the Navajos. He immediately challenged the terms of the treaty, including the amount of land to be received and the boundaries specified. The identified area did not include some ancestral lands such as Dinétah and the Chaco region. The tribe was then told that they would be paid for these exclusions. Finally, on July 18, 1855, the treaty was signed. Congress never ratified it.

The Navajos were still self-sufficient, although this ability had been negatively affected by the ongoing warfare with the New Mexicans and the Americans. The tribe was largely pastoral, although they did plant a few thousand acres annually and irrigate them. They lived mainly by maintaining large flocks and herds of sheep, goats, and horses, and were very resourceful in caring for themselves. As the century progressed this self-sufficiency gradually decreased in direct relation to their dealings with the U.S. government.

The years between late-1855 and 1864 are remembered for intermittent raids from the Utes, Paiutes, Comanches, Kiowas, Puebloans, and New Mexicans. Crop production was next to nothing in those years because Navajo fields were continuously being destroyed.

Escalation of Navajo confinement at Fort Sumner was undoubtedly influenced by the death of Zarcillos Largos, who preceded Manuelito as the principal spokesperson for the tribe. Although Zarcillos Largos expressed his grief about his own relatives held as slaves in New Mexican households, he still advocated peace between the Navajos and New Mexicans. He was killed by New Mexicans traveling with Zunis in 1860.

A new Indian policy was then introduced in which the Apaches and their kindred, the Navajos, would be rounded up and confined to a single reservation, despite the fact that they had fought one another intermittently for years. The plan included making the Navajos and Apaches "Christian" and "farmers." It was not a new idea, as it was tried on virtually all of the tribes in their contact with the government. The Navajo place of confinement was to be Fort Sumner, or Hweldi, as the Navajos called it.

Military expeditions and slave raids had combed the mountains and deserts for Navajos prior to 1846. The people had become increasingly hemmed in. As much as one-third of the tribe may have already been in captivity as slaves for the New Mexicans, or for other tribes. The people had plunged to an all-time low in their history. Then Rope Thrower, or Kit Carson, who was also called Red Clothes, entered the picture. He first attacked the (Mescalero) Apaches under explicit orders that "All Indian men of the tribe are to be killed whenever and wherever" found. Rounding up the Apaches did not take too long and over four hundred were confined at Fort Sumner by March 1863. This accomplished, Rope Thrower entered Navajo country.

It began on July 1, 1863 in a gloomy time when the Navajos were hungry and weak. Because of this critical condition, Rope Thrower felt assured that it would only be a matter of time before the people would begin to starve, if they had not reached that stage already. In a final act of desperation, they would come in to him. He was partially right, most of the people did do that. He hounded them unmercifully, burning their hogans and fields and killing all livestock, leaving nothing untouched for the people to subsist on or return to. As the people fled their homes, they watched the destruction from a safe distance. When winter arrived, Rope Thrower stayed in pursuit of the people, determined to keep them running and to never allow them to rest or build strength. The people were weary, cold, and hungry. Many were ill. The weak began to die off first. Others began to think of surrender, even though many were shot on the spot as they tried to do this.

Canyon De Chelly, with its sheer red cliffs that climb to heights of one thousand feet, had become a refuge to the Navajos. They knew it well. In the canyon and its tributaries, the people were able to live off a variety of plants and crops, and there was water. En masse, the people converged on the canyon. They climbed the red walls to wait on precarious ledges that barely shielded them against the army, which they knew would certainly follow. The people watched the complete burning of the earth and destruction of anything edible. They had become emaciated, mere skeletons of a people. In small groups, they began to surrender. Finally, in March 1864, over one hundred Navajos started the Long Walk to Hweldi. The walk took about three weeks.

Thousands were to follow, with one-third never returning to Navajo country again. But Rope Thrower did not succeed in rounding up the entire tribe. A few thousand escaped. These were groups in Utah and eastern Arizona. Several Navajos fled to their kin, the (Chiricahua) Apaches, and a few were taken in by the Havasupai.

The Navajos claim that the buzzards and coyotes followed the long columns of people to Fort Sumner because death was so rampant among them. In the course of their journey, many children were stolen by New Mexican slave raiders while the army either ignored this or were helpless to stop it. Once there, the people decreased in number even more and had to endure other indignities.

Fort Sumner had been constructed on lands and war trails of the Comanches. With Navajo relocation, the people were constantly exposed to a powerful old foe. Comanche raids did not cease or bypass the land simply because Fort Sumner now stood there. The Navajos were provided no arms with which to defend themselves, and during the four-year confinement they lost countless people and livestock to New Mexican and Comanche raids.

Disease, such as smallpox and pneumonia, infested the fort, while the crops were destroyed by insects. There was famine and drought in a land with precious little drinking water. River water was unpotable, but the people drank it and became ill. Wood for construction, heat, and cooking was extremely limited. The supply was quickly used for building purposes. The Navajos found it necessary to dig mesquite roots for firewood and carry them on their backs for distances of several miles to their families. When the people had first arrived at Hweldi, many had constructed hogans in which to live, but as firewood was depleted, they began to burn the wood which made up their homes. Without homes, the people dug holes in the sandy earth, put a covering over the top, and lived in these holes throughout their stay at Fort Sumner. In addition to all of this, the Navajos still had to contend with the government that had placed them there. Because their confinement occurred during the Civil War, the Navajo difficulties were often very low on the list of government priorities. When monies were allocated to the Navajos, it was insufficient, and government graft and corruption guaranteed that what little money there was decreased considerably as it was passed from office to office and person to person. Food supplies often did not arrive on a regular basis, while spoiled food that was designated not acceptable for the soldiers to eat was given to the starving Navajos.

In November 1865, the Apaches at Fort Sumner wanted no more and they simply left. Some of the Navajos managed to escape too. It is interesting to note that many times Navajo men slipped in and out of Fort Sumner to return to Navajo country and check on relatives who had escaped Hweldi. Then the men returned to the fort to go on raids into Comanche country, bringing food and other plunder, having never been missed.

Of the nine thousand Navajos who went to Hweldi, approximately two thousand died there. This does not include the number who died enroute. Another one thousand people arrived there but then disappeared. Either they escaped or were lost to the numerous raiding parties invading the fort.

The people were constantly yearning for Diné Bi Keyah, Navajoland, after their arrival at Hweldi. Things did not improve for the Navajo in their confinement, and controversy grew in government circles over the deplorable conditions at Fort Sumner. Now apparent to many that Fort Sumner was a grotesque failure, it was a source of great embarrassment to the government.

Rumors spread among the Navajos that they would be sent to Indian Territory, or Wide Plains as they called it. A group of headmen were invited to visit it, but they declined. Barboncito, the headman who was predominant at Fort Sumner, replied to this: "When the Navajos were first created, four mountains and four rivers were pointed out to us, inside of which we should live. I hope you will not ask me to go to any other country except my own, it might turn out to be another Hweldi."

The survivors of Fort Sumner returned to their old homeland under the Treaty of 1868, unlike most tribes who were never permitted to return to the ancestral homelands they had previously claimed. But their reservation was now reduced about ninety percent from their original claim, and excluded Dinétah. The proposed reservation was three and a half million acres. The treaty contained a provision for heads of families to select tracts of land not exceeding 160 acres within the reservation, if they desired. Under its terms, "seeds and agricultural implements" were to be distributed besides clothing and other miscellaneous items. Sheep and goats would also be given to them in addition to "five hundred beef cattle and a million pounds of corn." Education was stipulated, with the government providing teachers and schoolhouses. But the thorny question of when Navajo slaves might be returned to the tribe went unanswered, though Barboncito plaintively related that "over half the tribe" were still bound by slavery.

It is well-known that when the people returned to Navajo country, many elders wept, so overcome were they by the site of the homeland and their sacred mountain. It was enough for the moment to be there. Later there would once again be hunger, for the livestock and food promised the people in the Treaty of 1868 took months to arrive.

The Navajos who never went to Fort Sumner began to surface, taking the returning people in and feeding them. But those who had remained did not consider themselves as having been defeated because they had never surrendered. As a result, they did not feel compelled to comply with the 1868 treaty.

When food and supplies were not brought for the newly released Navajos, it was inevitable that bands of raiders, especially the young men, began to slip away, foraging for food and stock to keep the people fed. Sheep and goats were eventually distributed, and it is said among the Navajos today that the wealthy Navajos at the turn of the past century were those people who managed to keep from eating their meager flock, though hunger was always with the people for the first few years.

Fort Sumner was a tragic experience for the people, but it is now more than one hundred years behind them. There was much death at the fort, but even during that dark time, the people gave birth and remembered who they were. In spite of these hardships and many other trials, the Navajos live on. The Navajo Reservation is currently twenty-four thousand square acres, overlapping into the states of New Mexico, Arizona, and Utah. By legislation over the years, land has been exchanged and added to the boundaries described in the Treaty of 1868, though the Dinétah area still remains apart from the Reservation. While the revered headmen, the likes of Narbona, Manuelito, Barboncito, Zarcillos Largo, and Ganado Mucho are now gone, the Navajos are plentiful, having multiplied until they are now the largest tribe in the United States.

* * *

In a tiny community in Arizona, below the Chuska Mountains, lie the remains of ancient people whom the Navajos call "enemy ancestors," the Anazasi. Just when they arrived and began to build their dwellings is difficult to say, and they disappeared as mysteriously as they arrived. Ruins of the Anazasi are numerous but are often hidden, perched on ledges that sing with the wind. Other ruins also exist among those of the Anazasi, from more recent times when the Navajos were being pursued by the Spaniards and Mexicans, and then by the American military expeditions.

The Navajo remains conceal stone axes, burned small-eared corn, pottery shards, animal and human bones. One such place is a mesa that rises several hundred feet into the Arizona sky. On the very top still stands a weather-beaten hogan with fortress walls to make access even more difficult. It was here that a vivid encounter between the Navajos and their aggressors, who were in pursuit of them, is still recalled.

Though it would be difficult to say with certainty when the incident occurred, it was during the period when the Navajos were constantly running from the slave expeditions. There were men, women, and children in the Navajo party, numbering fewer than one hundred people. The Navajo group had skirted around the mesa for several days trying to avoid capture, and in desperation, they decided to ascend it. To reach the top successfully required climbing aids, though there were a few nearly smooth hand- and toeholds, used much earlier by the agile Anazasi.

The mesa was less than a mile long and much narrower, but it offered the only available defense. While up there the people lived off small game and drank the clear water that had been caught in natural red rock bowls. But the water was limited, and soon most of the game had been snared. The people prepared and subsisted on a weak soup for as long as possible. Finally, they did not have even that. From their fortified location, they saw the Mexicans set up camp below the mesa. They camped there for several days. One day the Mexicans packed up and cleared out. The Navajos had been in the habit of posting a dog at the incline up the mesa. When the Mexicans departed, the Navajos failed to put the guardian there. Under the cover of darkness, the Mexicans returned and started to climb the mesa. But their progress was slow because they were carrying packs. They clumsily ascended, one at a time.

The Navajos had to escape so they made a daring plan. There was only one point on the mesa that was not as steep as the other sides, and that was a drop of several hundred feet. As the people saw it, they had no choice but to try it. Through the long night, the people fashioned a crude rope of an odd assortment of items and secured it at the southeast rim. As the raiders climbed up the northeast side of the mesa, the Navajos were carefully climbing down the rope on the other side. By the time the sun had risen a few inches off the ground, the people were safely at the bottom, but not without two casualties: A woman who carried a baby in a cradleboard on her back had plunged to her death. The people fled southward into a narrow canyon. There they waited above the walls that came closer and closer together.

Once on top of the mesa, the Mexicans were angered to see the people slip away from them again. They began to yell at them, and they saw where the people were headed. They would follow.

The Navajos had counted on it and had prepared a welcome for them. The Mexicans, riding mules, entered the canyon fearlessly and did not seem to notice that the canyon became deeper, that the walls closed in on them. At a given signal, the Navajo men showered them with boulders and logs that came rolling over them. The avalanche fell on its intended target.

In the Navajo group there were those who knew Spanish, having served as slaves in Spanish and New Mexican households. It is said among the Navajos that during this deadly shower many of the assaulted men cried, calling out to the Navajos, "Diné! Diné!" Most of the Mexicans were killed instantly, but a few escaped and later returned to retrieve their dead. This place is called Where The Mexicans Cried, or Mexican Cry, among the Navajos.

There is a wooden marker at Where the Mexicans Cried, denoting the place where Nakai Nez Bitsilly, translated as Tall Mexican's Brother, rests. He was born in the 1850s and was a member of the Many House Clan. As a boy of almost seven, he was captured and went to Fort Sumner. It was at Hweldi that his father died of a disease the Navajos called the Big Sores.

Shortly before he was taken prisoner he was living with his mother in Canyon De Chelly. Since there were rumors of soldiers in the immediate vicinity, the people took care to be alert and prepared for an encounter or skirmish with them. But the people were also celebrating the successful harvesting of their crops, particularly because in previous years their harvests were meager or nonexistent. A feast was in preparation, and a festive mood prevailed. Nakai Nez Bitsilly later told his grandchildren that he ate and then went to gather wood from beyond a bend in the canyon. A few minutes later, his arms filled with the load of wood, he started back toward the people. He then heard the sound of gunfire cracking through the canyon. People began to scatter in all directions, and he could see men on horseback galloping down the canyon. They were soldiers and Ute scouts.

He dropped the bundle of firewood and crawled into a clump of bushes where he waited the entire day until it grew dark. When darkness fell, he came out of the bushes and began to make his way up the deep slopes. He said he wept as he made his escape, silently so the soldiers would not hear him. He didn't know if his mother was alive, but he doubted it. He slowly left the canyon, walking eastward toward the Chuska mountains. He was hungry but lived off seeds, cactus, and small game. In the Chuskas, several days later, he thought he heard a bell. He followed the sound and came upon a flock of sheep. A goat with a bell dangling from its neck was in the flock. The flock seemed to be on their own, but soon a woman made her presence known and told the boy that the sheep and goats belonged to her. They kept each other company for a few days, as she was in pretty much the same predicament that he was in, and she was kind and compassionate to him. When he was hungry, she milked goat's milk into his hands. On cold nights the woman undid a side of her woven dress that draped over her shoulders. He slept inside the dress with the woman.

Finally they met other Navajos, including his mother. Soon after, when a large group of people were herded to Fort Sumner, he was among them, along with his mother, father, and uncle. His memories of Fort Sumner included digging tunnels into the earth for firewood. On one such occasion when he was in the company of another boy about his age, the Comanches swooped down on the boys as they were tunneling some distance from the Navajo camp. He was digging deep in the tunnel while his friend was at its entrance. He heard the hooves of horses approaching. Only his friend was visible to the Comanches, and he heard him cry out. He began to fling sand over himself lest one of the Comanches look deeper into the tunnel. He saw his friend lifted up on the horse and heard him weep as he was quickly carried away. He was sure his friend would tell the Comanches that he was not alone, but his friend did not reveal this. He said he hid in that tunnel all day because he feared the Comanches were waiting for him to show himself.

His uncle, while at Fort Sumner, frequently went on raids against the Comanches for horses and other necessities. All of this happened under the sometimes unseeing eye of the government. He presumed his uncle was killed on such a raid since the last time he ever saw him was when his uncle had requested that the boy accompany this particular Navajo raiding party. He was told to practice with his bow and arrows because he would be carrying the food for the older men. For some reason, though, he did not leave with the raiding party and his uncle did not return. Similarly, the Comanches slipped in among the Navajo camps and helped themselves to a few horses. This, in turn, necessitated more raids into Comanche country.

Illnesses such as dysentery, Comanche raiding parties, plus the hunger at Fort Sumner, were the main things Naikai Nez Bitsilly remembered. There was one other thing he often described with melancholy and regret. He said that hunger was so prevalent, at times the soldiers would visit Navajo families and offer extra rations in exchange for one of the families' daughters. He said he and other boys came upon the Navajo girls and soldiers at the river. Much later, Bitsilly claimed that the reason the Navajos were having such hard times in his lifetime was "because we did everything there" (at Hweldi).

Naikai Nez Bitsilly survived Fort Sumner and returned to Navajo country. He was issued five goats and began the old Navajo life again. His mother remarried and died in childbirth after their return.

When Naikai Nez Bitsilly was about eighteen, he was on his way to the Chuska Mountains to do some hoeing. He had sharpened his hoe and climbed on his mule. Along the way, the mule spooked for some reason, and Nakai Nez Bitsilly fell on the sharpened hoe. He injured his back severely, maybe even broke it. In any case, the people had ceremonies for him, but he did not recover and it looked as if he might die. So the people built him a brush shelter and moved him outside the hogan and left him there, though they continued to take care of him as best they could. A medicine woman, who was his aunt, heard about him, stayed with him, and nursed him back to health. He recovered but was left with a limp. As a result, he was also called Limper.

Years after the Navajo police had been formed on the reservation, initially to curb the raids that continued after Fort Sumner, Naikai Nez Bitsilly joined this force. In this association he came to be known as Old Policeman.

In middle age, a little past the turn of the century, he married Hoskon Tsosie's Daughter. She was fifteen-years old, a member of the Jemez Clan, or Maii Deeshigiizhinii, and was born about 1888.

There are several versions of the origin of this clan. According to some Navajos, the Maii Deeshigiizhinii were derived from another clan called the Salt Clan, and so it follows that the two are closely related. The clan came into being at a lean time when the Navajos did not have any food. So the Navajos, members of the Salt Clan, decided to trade a young girl, about the age of eight, for corn—which was planted and eaten. The corn was traded for the girl with the people of the Jemez Pueblo. Later on, the Salt Clan people went to retrieve the girl, paying for her in corn again. By then the girl had children of her own, and they became the first of the Maii Deeshigiizhinii Clan.

Hoskon translates to mean Yucca Fruit, and Tsosie is Thin. Hoskon Tsosie and a woman simply called Dezba were the parents of Hoskon Tsosie's Daughter. Dezba had a grown daughter from a previous marriage, and Hoskon Tsosie married both the mother and daughter, which was a practice at the time. Dezba's mother was called Nazba, and her father was called Hunter. It is said that Hunter could communicate with the animals, calling them to him as he desired.

Naikai Nez Bitsilly and Hoskon Tsosie's Daughter stayed married for the rest of his life, until he died in old age in 1948. He was then buried Where The Mexicans Cried, though it was Hoskon Tsosie's Daughter's ancestors who were originally from the area. Naikai Nez Bitsilly was born near Sanostee, New Mexico.

Hoskon Tsosie's Daughter died in 1986. She lived a very active life, herding her small flock of sheep near the place Where The Mexicans Cried. She was a tiny woman who had been profoundly durable. In a small but strong voice, she told her great-great-grandchildren that her mother's name was simply Dezba, meaning Going To War. Her mother's mother was Nazba, Been To War. Before that time, she explained in Navajo, "People were different and did not have names as they do today."

A few feet from Hoskon Tsosie's Daughter's hogan is the home of one of her daughters. This daughter is the eldest offspring of her union with Old Policeman. The daughter, Nazba, is over seventy. Nazba married a Navajo man who grew up beside the San Juan River at a place called Cudei. As a child he was called Short Hair's Grandson. He is from the family of Sandoval, a Navajo headman who lived along the San Juan, not to be confused with other Sandovals.

Short Hair's Grandson's father was married twice and had two names: Hosteen Grey Canyon, for the place where he lived, and Short Hair Begay, meaning Short Hair's Son. Needless to say, Short Hair was one of the first Navajo men to wear his hair cut short. Short Hair's Grandson's mother was Short Hair's second wife. Short Hair's father was called Half-Fingers. He shot his thumb while hunting and sliced the finger off afterward because it just hung loosely on his hand.

Short Hair's Grandson is also a descendent of Tsii Baligaii through his mother. White Hair was a Ute who led many raids into Navajo country prior to Fort Sumner. His band roamed as far west as the Navajo Mountain area to the San Juan River, and into the Chuska Mountains. White Hair was notorious among the Navajos and his depredations were unforgivable to many. He was involved in an incident now called The Killing Of The Yei-bei-chai, Yei-bei-chai being the holy people of the Navajos. Another infamous act still recounted is the killing of a pregnant Navajo woman. As an example to the Navajos, and to convey his hostility toward them, it is claimed that he cut her open, and took out her baby. Then he slit out the baby's heart and placed it on an arrow which he shot into a raven's nest lodged in some trees. Most of the Navajos never forgave him for this act, but one Navajo woman bore children with him.

From the marriage of Nazba and Short Hair's Grandson came many children. Most of their children married Navajos, but three did not. The name Walters was recently acquired, taken from a family in Colorado. When the Navajo were first included in the census, the family's name would have been Begay. Nearly all the Navajo males used it for their names. The censustakers objected to so many Begays and suggested that the people adopt another name. For the family of Short Hair's Grandson the name Walters was selected. When Short Hair's Grandson took the name Walters for his family, one of his brothers decided to use it too.

One son of Nazba and Short Hair's Grandson married out of the Navajo Tribe and into the far away tribes of Wide Plains, or Oklahoma. Then from this union came two more grandchildren, great-grandchildren of Hoskon Tsosie's Daughter. But this time the great-grandchildren are a little different because they are a new combination of tribes—the Pawnee, the Otoe-Missouria, and the Navajo. And they live in a time of outer-space probes and high technology, and rock music. The great-grandchildren also go to college and have their own children. Both married Navajo women who bring into the family still another perspective on Navajo experience.

The great-great-grandchildren are another beginning and are yet a part of the same song the people have sung, of tribal and collective identity held since the dawn of time. So the great-great-grandchildren, by their very presence, sing with the wind the old stories and songs of humankind.

The Fourth World

The hills in Oklahoma have given birth many times. I was born there in what was once a part of the old Cherokee Strip. Then as a baby, my grandmother (father's mother) stole me away from my mother for a few year years. Later, when consciousness of life dawned on me, I was with the Otoe people.

For a while I thought the whole world was Indian, was Otoe. They opened my eyes and formed my first words with me. No, they did not put words into my mouth, and even if they did, I did not taste them. They filled my mouth and belly with wild berries me and Grandpa picked from a slow moving wagon. They filled me with fried bread, which widens the smile and waist. They filled me with old dreams they or their ancestors had dreamed collectively hundreds of years before. They made me see things only I could see, and hear the old stories and songs they told with exaggerated animation and sang with such haunting emotion. Maybe that is the same thing as putting words into my mouth. And they gave me things, all intangible things they had held in store for me—tingling warmth in my soul, an ancient view of the world, and a gnarled old hand to reach out to. Then they left me on this plane of time, standing by myself, but far from being alone. They put questions in my brain and left me dazzled, their images blew me promises like kisses thrown across the room. Yes, it may be that is the same thing as putting words into my mouth.

The Otoe-Missouria Tribe had been in the hills some sixty-five years by then. They had put up buildings on the land, but the buildings confined the people and they spent most of their time under the sun, the stars, and the clouds. They had grown familiar with the land, the draining heat of summer, the herbs that grew in the tall grass, and the tribes surrounding them, such as the Pawnees.

Actually, the two tribes had had contact with each other for several centuries and knew each other well, having had warfare with one another and at other times having been allies. The Pawnees had been removed only four or five years before the Otoe-Missouria, and the tribes had experienced many of the same things in the transition process. Both tribes had left sacred and secret places known only to them in Nebraska. It had affected them deeply, despite the fact that they brought with them what they could: the languages, the songs, the customs, and some ceremonies. The Otoe-Missouria had always been a small tribe and their size was something they accepted. The Pawnees, on the other hand, had been a numerous people, reduced considerably in size in just a few years time. It happened too quickly for the people to make proper adjustment, so that their ceremonial life had been greatly disturbed and they would never completely recover from the loss. Many of the tribe's healing and other societies disintegrated when members passed away in large numbers, too swiftly for someone else to have been designated or trained to take the missing member's place. The people always deferred to the prescribed rituals that membership in these societies required, and they were, consequently, at a loss when they could not fill the empty seats in those societies. Ceremonial life continued, but it had suffered drastically by the turn of the last century.

The Pawnee Agency was located about thirty miles from the Otoe-Missouria headquarters, and it eventually served both tribes, along with the Ponca Tribe situated directly north of the Otoe-Missouria Tribe. There was also a boarding school in Pawnee that was created by treaty and served these three tribes and others.

Though the Otoes would never become the farmers the government desired, the people did have an affinity for the land, and in time, places in Oklahoma would become as dear to them as the ones they had left in Nebraska.

Perfectly shaped hills that looked as if some gentle and patient fingers had molded them lay around our people. Creeks curled through the hills, rising a natural high, and became muddy red after the rains when the creekbeds filled with life and spilled over. The smell of dirt washed clean rose in the thick air and made people crave for the taste of it. The trees along the creekbanks were huge roots turned upside-down with hanging vines that half a dozen raggedy little children clung to as they swung recklessly from limb to limb.

The house we lived in was once white. The sun, wind, and rain unpainted it to a splinter gray. It stood in the center of a bowl. Inside the wooden structure were six rooms. Doors were to the east and south. The south opened to an indoor porch area. There was an old refrigerator for block ice as well as an assortment of odds and ends stored there: harnesses, a washboard, picks, a hat, a wash basin with an aging yellow bar of soap. In the middle of that room, hidden under torn linoleum, was a door in the floor that could be lifted up. This was a secret storage place that was used to stash precious things when the house was empty. Next to this room was a small bedroom with a window facing west, where Grandpa passed several times a day, doing his chores and leading the workhorses from the fields to the workshed or barn, and back again.

A big black wood stove stood in the kitchen. A long buffet table was at the kitchen door, and near it, a heavy circular wooden table that would seat about ten people. It held the meals that fed the family and the community, who rode in by wagon, or walked several miles, to tell Grandpa and Grandma about the tribal doings at the agency locale, or of the tribe's most recent death. The guests then retreated to the living room, next to the kitchen, and talked with serious faces about what was happening in these times, in faraway Washington, and how actions there would affect the people here.

The last bedroom in the house belonged to Grandma and Grandpa. Above the doors were fastened Grandpa's canes. He broke a leg in his youth and it healed crookedly, forcing him to use a cane. A pot-bellied stove warmed this room. There were huge trunks in the corner. Thick quilts were spread on the double bed. Grandma had made the quilts with patches of her life—faded wool and worn blue jeans. For a couple of years I slept between Grandma and Grandpa under those heavy covers and heavy dreams. They would leave to go to the kitchen for coffee and to visit with returning children who came to tell the old folks how life was being lived in other places, while Grandma and Grandpa sat patiently telling them of Otoe life by repeating stories beside the wood stove in winter or under the stars in warm weather. They left me with the flicker of red flames, wood crackling in the night, and shadows of myself and them dancing across the dim room.

One night I awoke in that dark old house and realized I was alone. I was in the living room and remembered that this wasn't where I had gone to sleep, between Grandma and Grandpa. Someone had moved me. I got up to peek at the rooms in the house. All was black, except in their room. Light seeped through the bottom of the door. I tiptoed quietly, lifting my head to listen for them. Then a thought rushed across my mind that maybe I should not do what I was planning to do. After all, someone had moved me outside. I pushed the door quietly nonetheless. It resisted a little, but I managed to see anyway.

Grandpa was without a shirt, sitting on the floor. He sighed and sang softly, almost inaudibly. The lamp was dim and came from their right. Light bounced off the sides of them and stretched the shadows across the floor. Grandma sat behind Grandpa on her knees. She was cleaning Grandpa's back. Grandma then took a knife and gracefully made several cuts an inch or so long and apart from each other. Blood began to slowly drip from the incisions and trickle down his skin. Grandma took a horn and applied the large end to the cut on his back. She placed the other end in her mouth and drew blood from his back, then spit it in a container to her side.

Both Grandma and Grandpa were unusual people. They possessed precious knowledge of now forsaken things. And they saw the world in other dimensions than what we are taught to see today.

The next morning I awoke between them after having gone back to sleep on the couch. I knew instinctively that they were aware of my presence at their door, but they did not scold me or speak of the night before. That wasn't their way. Besides, if one looked around the Otoe world there were better reasons for anger.

Grandpa Tom, who reared me, was a full-blood Otoe, and it was said during his lifetime that he was one of a very few whose blood ran true. He was born about 1873. His own father was in middle age when Grandpa arrived. His mother was about twenty years older than Grandpa.

Grandpa was a man who could be uncompromisingly stern and yet behave like a clown. He felt words the way you feel the wind when it sings above. Grandpa touched time the way he touched a wound, sensitive to it but probing. He often took the mysterious world apart with his bare hands and laughed at the mystery—it was the ultimate explanation. He laughed at everything: protocol and Washington; at everybody, including kin; and he laughed best at himself. He had the power to make everyone at ease with his sly smiles after he did something unexpected, such as irreverently pulling the world apart in front of awestruck eyes. Then he would calmly put the world back together again, stand off, and admire his handiwork—and he would laugh. I noticed, too, that most of the times we parted from him, he was laughing.

Within certain tribes, including the Otoe, one does not speak to or communicate with their in-laws. It happened that when my mother went home with my father, Grandpa Tom was always around. He knew some Pawnee language because he was once married to a Pawnee woman. He also knew some Pawnee songs and favored the ones from the Ghost Dance. As Mom and Grandpa became comfortable with one another, there was a mutual respect between them, but neither ventured beyond the boundaries that had previously been drawn.

After Mom had been with the family for a while, she noticed that Grandpa would do things which provoked her, but she was always uncertain how she might respond. When Mom was alone, for example, Grandpa took to being nearby, often singing Pawnee songs, appearing to talk to himself using Pawnee expressions. He would slyly watch Mom to see how she reacted to this, a smile playing over his face. But by the time Mom had finally decided on action, she looked at him and his face was completely blank, as if he had never said or done anything. He appeared to be very serious about their in-law relationship. Grandpa's behavior was distracting for my mother who tried her best to maintain a respectful attitude toward the in-law custom, all the while attempting to assert herself and earn a place in this tribe whose customs and rules varied from the Pawnee's. She was young and wanted to impress Grandpa and his family, but she had been instructed to more or less ignore him and go about her own business. Grandpa, being Grandpa, made it trying.

One evening at the supper table, Grandpa went into a long recitation concerning his childhood. Seemingly to nobody in particular, he stated very seriously, "Bah, I remember when I was a baby." His recollection was really directed to my mother, in a respectable roundabout way. He sort of tossed out this information at the table and left it for the others, who took what they wanted with their meal. Everyone continued to eat as they listened. The whole family knew he was teasing my mother, although she was unaware of it yet. He was daring her to react to him, her in-law.

He said, "Bah, I remember when I was little. You know I was only a baby, but I can remember back then. I remember that one time everybody went on a hunt. They stood me up on the ground in the cradleboard. I leaned against a tree. Everybody was hunting. They went to hunt rabbits.

"Bah, I saw a lot of rabbits. They went right by my cradleboard. I wanted to call out and tell someone, but bah . . . I was just a little baby and I hadn't learned how to talk."

Silence. Grandpa waited. Without expression, he played with his food. Nothing came from my mother. She stared around the room, trying not to look at Grandpa, trying not to smile. But he had told a silly tale, and she began to giggle. My father had watched from the side and kicked my mother's foot under the table.

"You are not supposed to laugh at him!" My father said to her.

"Don't notice him."

My mother stole a glance at Grandpa. He had turned away from her. His face was buried in his hands and his shoulders were moving up and down in silent laughter. He wrapped his arms around his waist and laughed and laughed. He didn't make a sound though. Just as abruptly, he stopped his antics and went back to his plate. Both Grandpa and Mom acted as if the other were not at the same table, let alone the same house! They often took pains to give the respectful impression that they were unaware of each other.

How could anyone not be aware of Grandpa? Everyone knew him, yet no one did. There are those who perceived him differently—his own children, his parents, historians.

The land, the house, Grandma, and I belonged to Grandpa briefly. We spent the days walking along the banks of the creek called Greasy Creek. I remember redbud trees in the spring, and Grandpa. I remember cotton fields on the northside of the house, and Grandpa. I remember a dank cellar stuffed with ripe, pungent foods, and Grandpa. I remember wild plum bushes, and Grandpa. I remember crispy cold mornings, and Grandpa.

Every day that old man held a little girl in his lap and sang a song for her. Sometimes the weight on his lap would cause discomfort in his leg and he would shift her to his feet. Holding his legs straight in front of him, feet on the floor, he made a chair for her to sit on. He would then sing his song for her. It was a song that called her by name and said how she liked fried bread. He sang other Otoe songs with his hand drum. He gently pounded his right fist into his left palm.

Grandpa kept many animals around the house: cows, horses, chickens, cats, and especially dogs. At times he had as many as a dozen dogs. I believe this was due partly to his recollection of the dogs following the people from Nebraska, for Grandpa was the child who witnessed the event. He felt a very real bond for all life forms, the seen and the unseen. He had an overwhelming compassion for strays—animals, people, and especially children.

It was during this haunting time that I thought the whole world was Indian. There was no reason yet to think otherwise. There was a time, indeed, when my world really was Indian. It revolved around Grandpa. Oh, Grandpa was young then, and I was old. We rode time like it was his own wagon. It left splinters in my hands.

Then Grandpa fell ill. He was taken to the Pawnee Indian hospital. He waved to all his grandchildren standing outside the hospital below the window in his room. Of course the hospital did not allow children inside. When Grandpa did not get better, however, the hospital staff relented. I saw Grandpa die in his bed by the window.

His body was brought home to us in the custom of the Otoes and rested in a gray coffin that was put in the living room. People came in from the hills of Otoe country to pay proper respect to "old man." They entered the house, looked at him, and then sat up with him for three nights. During that time, individuals stood to give their knowledge of "old man," to reflect on his character and the manner in which he lived his life. This took place in front of him and his relatives where all might hear. There were Otoe songs that could be heard in the back room where I lay, where Grandpa used to sleep. In the daytime there was more company, and we children passed Grandpa's coffin not at all fearful of him in death.

The Otoes reasoned that when an individual passes away, his spirit wanders to his closest kin as a gesture of farewell before the spirit departs. His body was kept in the house in order for friends and relatives to reciprocate.

South of the house the land sloped down to the creek. Relatives camped under the trees at Grandpa's death. Women aided Grandma and the aunts in various tasks. One was to feed those people who came to sit up with Grandpa. On the morning of the fourth day, our family fed the entire Otoe tribe.

Following that was a "giveaway." Most of the Plains people practice this custom. Grandpa's articles of clothing and most of his possessions were distributed to close relatives and people he loved. What was not given away was destroyed by burning.

The Otoe people accompanied him to the cemetery and "put him away."

At the cemetery I was instructed by Grandma to walk over a plank that crossed the opening in the ground horizontally. His coffin had been let down beforehand. I threw a chunk of dirt into the earth as I stood on the plank, and then we left Grandpa there.

Grandma remained at the house. Her children objected because she was often alone. The house was miles away from town, and the neighbors had drifted off. It used to be that there were Otoe people in all directions, a whistle or a cry away. They were older people who had either gone the way of Grandpa, or else their houses had emptied with the children grown, and they followed the children rather than stay alone.

But nothing scared Grandma. She looked everything in the eye, not rudely but expectantly. It seemed as if Grandma was always expecting someone or something, constantly looking out the window or down the road.

Although Grandma Lena was by herself then, she had a strange strength and was very tough. Physically, she could take care of herself until the very end.

Grandma often worked alone in the buildings which stood on Grandpa's farm. She worked as a man works, lifting and carrying heavy loads. After a long day, when she came in to change her dress, as it lay there on the floor, amber scorpions crawled out to us children.

In the same sense that she was tough, Grandma was equally weak. Grandma wept easily. It was not for herself that she wept. She cried with people for people. If we cried, she helped us. She wept upon seeing someone she hadn't seen for a while. She cried with a person as they cried, even an infant.

Grandma did not cry out loud or whine or wail. She cried silent tears and caught them in her apron. Grandma was not ashamed to weep. Nor were other elders in the tribe, men and women.

In prayer or when listening to the prayers of another, the tears were always there in the peoples' eyes to support the words. Grandma wept when she prayed, or when she listened to someone else and they wavered in emotion. In fact, when Grandma participated in tribal "doings," the prayers were memorable. A person began to pray just as if he were speaking to someone in the room. He wept as he prayed to

Waconda, the Creator. Then another person began where he ended. The people prayed for everything in the world, from the tiny blades of grass, to the wind, the sun, the stars, the insects, fire, and water. If a person failed to mention something, another remembered until everything in the universe had been mentioned.

Just as true is that Grandma was a very proud and haughty lady. If she found something or someone unpleasant or disagreeable to her, she said so. She folded her arms in front of her, stuck out her chin defiantly, turned her head away from the source of her distaste, and say, "Humph!" through a closed mouth and pursed lips. No amount of budging could make her change her mind.

Whatever was on her mind to speak, and however she chose to illustrate her point, she did it graphically and purposefully. Grandma always made herself perfectly understood.

Grandma, like Grandpa, was a believer. She liked to believe. Grandma believed in everything, in all the churches, in the God of each. She knew that some things could not be satisfactorily accounted for, and she accepted those things.

There were times when I witnessed unusual incidents in her presence. I heard her talk to and address nothing that I could see. Several times I saw this old lady pucker up her face and wrap the apron around her hands, her only weapon. She talked to the night or the wind. She didn't speak hysterically or desperately. She spoke calmly and confidently, as if this were the only reasonable thing to do.

At night when the dogs howled wildly or barked at something, we young people became uncomfortable being by ourselves with Grandma. She would burn cedar and "smoke" our world, easing our minds. The Otoe believe that the scent of cedar has special properties. Grandma would comfort us with cedar and put our world in order. To this day, those of us who were there find that the scent of cedar permeates our lives.

At other times I saw her apologize to the night, to the wind, for being the intruder in their world, instead of the reverse. Grandma was not an ignorant woman. She often acknowledged the fact that she was not the only living being in this world and that there were many dimensions to it.

People like Grandma are often called superstitious or foolish for their beliefs. She knew that. Her philosophy was clean and simple, however. Whatever one says or does will make a circle and return to its origin in the manner it was extended. Others will give it back. Grandma had extraordinary faith, but she never attempted to convert us to her way of thinking, forcing it on us. She went her way with or without us. Usually, we followed not far behind her.

Grandma spent the days fishing alone. She walked to one of the nearby ponds or creeks. She tried to keep the farm going for a while after Grandpa died, but it was too much for her so she spent her time sewing, cooking, cleaning, and fishing.

Grandma was a familiar figure to the Otoe people. She came from an old established family and was active in tribal affairs and society. She camped at all the encampments, taking her grandchildren with her. When Grandma was invited here and there, she did her best to attend and do those things expected of her.

In the evenings, she and I sat outside the house facing east. Every day a hawk came from that direction looking for his daily kill, and Grandma commented on it. She told long stories in a soft voice that carried through the hills.

Grandma was a diabetic. While she had knowledge of herbs and healing to a certain extent, diabetes was something else, a disease she knew little about except for the fact that it was directly responsible for the deaths of many Otoe people.

A small bruise rose on Grandma's foot, and it started to swell. She went to the hospital and came away with instructions to stay off the foot. They also gave her pills and insulin. The bruise did not respond to medication, and became sore like fruit that goes bad. Her foot grew to twice its size. The sore became infected and the ankle then began to swell. Grandma was hospitalized at this point, and the sore was drained and bandaged. It refused to heal. The leg, to the knee, began to swell. Finally, Grandma's leg was amputated above the knee. When Grandma was confined to a wheelchair, she let go of her world and removed herself from the mainstream of Otoe life.

Her children encouraged her to leave the old place and live with them. Grandma finally did this, but with many misgivings. The old house still stood, and as long as it did, Grandma came around in her wheelchair to help hold it up. Or, perhaps, they supported one another. In any case, she often talked about going down there for a while and even dreamed of staying there alone. Her children wouldn't hear of it. When Grandma was at the old house, she patted the cracking walls tenderly and picked up parts of the falling ceiling. Then she sat outside facing east like hundreds of times before, so quietly, so expectantly.

* * *

For many years Grandma Cora, Pawnee grandmother, was a distinguished woman. Being elderly and having established her place firmly in Pawnee society, she was a member of an elite group of old ladies who behaved as no other group could.

Grandma Cora was often amusing in this new role. She liked to walk. But not being as youthful or agile as she once was, she took little tiny steps getting to her destinations.

Grandma Cora was identifiable for a quarter of a century, along with many other elderly women, as one of those who walked all over Pawnee. In most cases these women could ride the distance if they desired, but they preferred to walk. They all were similar in dress, wearing toothless smiles, turban scarfs wound over their heads, and aprons over their skirts.

Somehow Grandma Cora always managed to get her tent at the Pow-wow grounds before we did. There, little children sneaked up behind her and pulled her skirts or apron strings. Grandma Cora jumped up and down and made faces at the little ones and pretended that she was going to catch them.

Grandma Cora had the use of only one eye. With it she saw through all of us.

The time came when Grandma no longer walked to the Pow-wow grounds, taking those little tiny steps we smiled about. Her limited sight had been dimming. She fell and broke her hip.

She was taken to the Public Health Service Hospital where she was examined, x-rayed, and then sent home. Hospital personnel said there was no damage. She walked about for over a week. At night she cried in pain. Uncle was with her and was very worried about her suffering. He said that there was indeed something damaged if she groaned constantly and hurt when she moved. He said that one need not be a doctor to see the condition she was in. One needed only eyes to see that.

Grandma was taken back to the hospital where her children insisted that she be reexamined. Grandma had a broken hip. By then the pain for a lady in her eighties was unbearable. She was nearly out of her mind from it. After the doctors verified the pain and the broken hip, they said that they could not fix Grandma. The strain would not be possible for her. It was too late.

Grandma was placed in a home for the elderly because of her need for professional care. Times for the Pawnees have surely changed. In another era this would not even have been considered. There, in the nursing home, Grandma was given some relief from the pain of the broken hip, though it never mended. So Grandma Cora, too, became confined to a wheelchair. Her brown skin faded into pale gold from lack of walking in the sun. Her hair became white and soft as downy feathers.

We visited her often. She was very alert but was extremely hard of hearing. In conversation she switched from English to Pawnee and back again.

* * *

I was the oldest child. For the first few years, I had lived with the old folks. About school age, I was returned to my parents to be placed in school. It was a traumatic experience.

By the third grade some changes came into me and my sisters' lives that happened very suddenly. There were three of us girls, and the youngest was nearly two years old. She had appeared to be well and was very intelligent. Everyone was so proud of her. This is when her long illness began, followed by our mother's. Tuberculosis was the same disease that killed her father and several relatives. She would be gone from us for nearly two years. We visited her at the hospital where the ward was filled with Indian people from several tribes, all suffering from the same disease. We could not touch our mother, and we all had to talk through little white masks over our mouths.

Our father tried to care for us by himself. He took us with him wherever he went, when it was possible. Sister and I followed him across the pastures and climbed through the fences to catch the buses that would take us to our mother, or into town. Sometimes we hitch-hiked with our father.

In this particular year, the time for school to start had passed, but sister and I were still at Grandma Lena's. She tried to keep us with her and said that she would find a way to send us to school while our father went off to work in town, but our father resisted, saying that we would be too much for Grandma. She was without transportation and getting on in years.

Finally, one day our father and grandmother called sister and me to them and explained that we were going to attend a different kind of school. They had enrolled us in a boarding school in Pawnee. This was the school provided by treaty obligation. We were Indians, and it was a school for us. Being reminded that we were Indian was one of the facts to which we would become increasingly exposed.

Grandma helped us pack our things, and sister and I were taken to the school and introduced to the matrons and administrative staff— and to a strange new experience. It was the first time in our lives that we were really separated from our parents and grandparents. Sister often stayed with Grandma Cora, as I had with Grandma Lena.

But this time we had no relatives with us, we were completely alone. At least we had each other for company. Some children did not have sisters or brothers there and were more alone than we were.

Sister had been named Gi-su, meaning Little, Round (fat), and Cute, by the Pawnees. Gi-su and I attended Pawnee Boarding School following the pattern set by our family. Grandma Cora and our mother had gone there too. During Grandma Cora's and our mother's stay there, the school was much stricter than in our time. When Grandma

Cora attended school, there was still bitter resistance to the idea of school because of what it represented, a foreign way of life. The people feared that the institution and the schooling process would be used against them, and their fears were later confirmed.

Most of the boarding schools in fact did attempt to take children from their Indian parents and transform them into "little white people." While at these schools, children were not permitted to leave the school grounds during a school term, even with their parents, lest the parent-child relationship destroy what the school had thus far accomplished. Children were absolutely forbidden to speak their native languages, and punishment for this offense varied with the person in charge. All students were required to attend "church" and were disciplined if they did not. All the schools were administered in a military fashion, with their recruits as young as five-years old. Many children had to endure this relationship for their entire schooling, from the first grade to whatever level they finally reached. Hundreds of students got out of school as quickly as possible by whatever means available. Years later, the government would initiate tedious and expensive studies on why Indian students failed or did not perform well in school. It was no wonder.

During Grandma Cora's school days, old Pawnee people taunted and bribed the youth to speak in Pawnee to them. They knew that eventually the people would forget the language. At the same time, the school staff and administrators, who in later years were Indians, would urge the students to forget their language and anything having to do with being Indian as quickly as possible. A few of these Indian staff members really believed that letting go of Indian identity was best for themselves. Others simply felt that maintaining tribal and Indian identity was a losing battle, and thus admitted defeat. It is interesting to note, however, that the Indian staff of the boarding schools had gone through the same schooling process that they later returned to administer.

Our mother's experience with school varied somewhat from Grandma's and ours, in that she came from a very impoverished family with Grandma Cora the head of the household. Grandma Cora provided for her family in the traditional Pawnee way, by attending all the Pawnee activities and offering her services to the people. She was often called upon to cook at these gatherings, or to help with the sick, etc. In a reciprocal gesture, the people cared for her and her family, by paying her in meals and with small materials and goods. Since that was the way in which Grandma Cora provided for her children, it required that she be on the move all the time, at the various camps of the Pawnees, and sometimes with other tribes. Consequently, the family lived in a tent year round during most of my mother's childhood. In winter, and when the snow fell, Grandma Cora still followed tribal activities and ceremonies. So our mother had this kind of life too, with many people looking out for Grandma Cora's children, as well as for Grandma.

Grandma Cora's life was drastically different from my mother's, in the sense that Grandma's life was very hard, working all the time to feed herself and her children. Being the daughter of Captain Jim, Grandma was welcome everywhere in the Pawnee community. While my mother was in attendance at ceremonial gatherings and activities when she was quite young, and saw a part of life that would one day be no more, Grandma, too, saw the signs, and wanted an easier life for our mother.

Though our mother is not inclined to reminisce on her youth often, there are rare moments today when she recalls and sings an old song for us that she suddenly remembers and is surprised that she knows. At times she becomes still and thoughtful and says something such as, "You know, sister, I remember something. I remember that Momma and I were at a camp somewhere, and Momma put me to sleep, then she left the tent. In the middle of night, I woke up and there was a woman sitting in the tent with me. She had long braids, and a blanket was draped over her shoulders. She was sewing. I went back to sleep. The next day I asked my mother, 'Who was that here last night?' And your grandmother said, 'No one was here. What did she look like?' I described the woman to her and my mother said, 'Oh, that sounds like so-and-so.' She gave me a name of a woman who hadn't lived for some years."

At other precious times our mother will comment on the Pawnee people during her childhood. "The people were still dancing the Ghost Dance when I was little. They used to dance at the old grounds outside of Pawnee. I really don't remember it too well, except that I can barely see them, moving with tiny steps in moccasined feet. Ask your Aunt."

Grandma took a bold step to assure that her children were fed: She put them in school. She did not delude herself about the logic of it. She did not say, "Master the three r's and return to help your people," as we hear so often today. What Grandma did say was, "In school you will eat three times a day and you will be clothed." Grandma put her children in school so that they might be *fed*. Life was desperate, and Grandma could barely provide the necessities for herself, let alone her children. During the lean times when there was absolutely nothing to eat, the family endured it until the next meal came. Grandma knew there were certain risks in sending the children to school. She knew that our mother might be seduced by it all. But Grandma cut the tie between her and our mother. Her daughter went off to school where they learned such things as how to pour tea gracefully, fold napkins and such, while Grandma continued to follow the camps, eking out her simple existence. But it was in a world that was familiar and dearly loved, for it was a Pawnee world, and Grandma was a Pawnee to her very soul.

By the time Gi-su and I went to boarding school, it was ostensibly more lenient with the students. At the beginning of the school year, we children were disinfected, sprayed, and bathed in bad-smelling solutions. Our heads were drenched in potions and I asked for what reason. The matrons replied that the school worried that we were filled with bugs and other nasty things, in our hair and on our bodies. I replied that I wasn't and never had seen such things on the people that I knew. But the matron assured us that some people wore those things. I was somehow insulted as I watched all the children being doused with the solution. Not too long afterward, someone clipped my braids below each ear, and I wailed to Gi-su over the loss of my prized braids. I kept the braids in a shoe box for the rest of the year until they were discovered and deposited in a trash can. There were other little girls who cried with me because our hair was cut. The matrons, in a way that was meant to be kind, told us that they didn't have time to help each of us dress and to comb our hair every morning. They said they had enough work to do, trying to oversee us, cleaning, etc. All of us students looked alike in our new haircuts, and when the school issued some clothing and shoes to us, we felt strange and different, seeing our look-alikes everywhere we turned.

Another thing the matrons conveyed to us very early in the game was the message that we ought to be grateful to be at the school which the government so graciously provided for us. We should be glad that there was this fine old institution which would take us in and delouse us, and cut our hair, and give us shoes, and feed us, and let us sleep in its army beds. It was a message we would hear repeatedly all our lives.

There were two dormitories at the school, one for the boys and one for the girls. All of us rose before dawn and had roll call outside the dorms every morning, rain or shine or snow. Roll call was done to see if anyone had run away in the night since the last roll call before going to bed. We did calisthenics for a few minutes, and then lined up and marched to the dining room. We marched all over Pawnee in the years we attended the boarding school. One of my jobs was to sweep the outside porch in the fall. It was an illogical assignment to my reasoning. As soon as I swept one place, the wind sang and the trees sighed while the leaves fell on the cement slab. I would stand and watch, imagining that I had to sweep the leaves of all the trees in the world.

The school served grades one to eight. Every morning began with a lecture on the privilege of going to class here, and every evening we were also reminded of our good fortune. We were urged to be cooperative with our teachers, submissive to the dorm matrons, and to "get along" with each other.

The students at the school were from many tribes and each child was thoroughly aware of old animosities among the tribes. It did present problems. The children had been well-versed in who their people were, what their people had accomplished, and how their respective people felt about other tribes. The Indian boarding schools operated on the premise that all the tribes were alike, and that children from many tribes would have to attend one school to save government money in school construction and maintenance. But the children knew that the tribes had different philosophical concepts, social relationships, and organization, and that certain tribes had fought each other since the beginning of time.

For instance, there were children who called all the Pawnees, "horse thieves" in their own language. Those children could tell stories and give locations where Pawnees had come into their tribe and taken all their tribe's horses. We Pawnee children knew that we were being called a derogatory name, and of course would have to make some reply which was appropriate to the history of another child's tribe. We knew that some tribes practiced sorcery, that others in the distant past had practiced cannibalism, that one of our ancestors had fought in face-to-face combat with another child's great-great-grandparent. There were many physical fights, and almost every child there participated at one time or another. Most of the Indian children who attended boarding school learned how to fight at an early age.

Then there were other times when we managed to slip away from the matron's eyes and be by ourselves, and we listened to the stories of each other's family and people that all of us told. We heard how so-and-so's grandmother could turn herself into a snake, how someone else's people were buried in trees, the stories of Deer Woman, and countless other tales.

In adjusting to the regimentation of boarding school life, my sister, who had so looked forward to going to school, now found it very trying. She'd never been to school and had never been away from our mother and father, or Grandma Cora. Early in the year she fell into the habit of wetting the bed. She had never done that before. The matrons at first were as patient as they could be. There were several other students beside Gi-su who did this. They helped sister change her sheets, and so forth. In fact, Gi-su and I never had to make our beds before or wash our own clothes until going to the school. But with each bed-wetting, the matrons began to lose their tolerance with Gi-su. They began to punish her, gave her more work assignments, and kept her from play. But none of this solved the problem. Her bed-wetting increased. Gi-su became kind of desperate, trying to hide her accidents in whatever way she could. Naturally, she was quite embarrassed, while the matrons began to make an example of her in the hopes that sister would control herself.

One morning, Gi-su was up about four, fully dressed and ready to start the day. Of course this made the matrons suspicious because all the other children were still asleep. That day one of the matrons came to my bed and got me. She explained to me that from then on, every time Gi-su wet the bed, she must wash her bedding by hand, by herself. When I saw Gi-su, she seemed dejected and worried. She was at the huge round sink that spanned an entire room, rubbing the sheets between her hands. She had to complete her unpleasant job before breakfast. I went over and helped her. What else could I do?

So for a few weeks following this decision, every morning on schedule, Gi-su and I did sister's laundry before breakfast. As winter came, there was frost in the air that we noticed when we took the dripping sheets out to hang on the clothesline behind our dormitory. Eventually, as days grew colder, the sheets froze and formed a layer of ice as soon as we stepped out the door. Finally, one blissful morning, her bed was dry and our early morning washing ended.

Actually, Gi-su had a rough time at school. In between her fights with other students, and the bed-wetting episode, she also had some bad experiences in the cafeteria. As we ate, the matrons walked from table to table, making certain that each of us ate everything on our plates that had been provided for us by the government. No one was allowed to dump any food in the trash can. One or two of the matrons force-fed Gi-su beets and other foods, holding her arms down, prying open her mouth and clenched teeth, and shoving food into her mouth. Gi-su spit it out, but each time it was shoveled back in until finally sister gave up and swallowed the mess.

Saturday, every two weeks, was town day. Boys and girls alternated. We marched to town and back, two by two. Often on the Friday before, Gi-su and I received a letter from our father with two crisp dollar bills inside. He wrote regularly, and his humorous letters were the envy of every girl there. We shared the letters with our friends and soon most of the dormitory residents waited as eagerly for the letters as we did. On Sunday, Grandma Lena visited us. I always begged to go home with her. She cried with me, though I eventually learned to control myself and never repeated the incident when I cried most of the day the first time we were deposited at school. Grandma Lena would always lie to me and say she had something else to do first and then would be back to get me. She never had the courage to tell me otherwise, or to stay away and not visit us. Every week it was the same story. Every week I believed it.

One of the things about boarding school that also left an impression on me was how the boys were punished for running away, or for violating one of many rules. The boys would have to go through a belt line, in which a student's peers would have the chance to whip the offending student.

Gi-su and I spent two years at the boarding school. Then our mother came home from the hospital. Our youngest sister, though, was nowhere near recovery. With our mother home, she and our father spent many trips trying to see our youngest sister. The hospital would only allow our parents to peer through windows and not let them inside. One day they told us that sister did not remember them at all. They said sister wore braces to her hips. When she finally came home, she didn't know any of us and studied our parents strangely, as if trying to remember them, or believe that she had parents.

By the fifth grade when we had moved to another town, I had become acutely conscious of subtle changes in my world. There were only a handful, perhaps a dozen, Indian students in the school we were attending. Everyone else's skin was white or black. The whites and the blacks fought each other, called each other the worst things they could think of, and made fun of each other when the opportunity arose. They rolled in the streets after school or during recess, pulled each other's hair, and bit each other viciously. The blacks and the whites often looked at us as if we were an enigma to them.

My teacher was kind in her own way, and was sincere enough. Every day, or at least every week, she said to the class, "We should bow our heads in shame for what we did to the American Indian." My classmates looked at me while she patted my head and said that I was her pretty little Indian girl. I hated her for doing that to me. It was a strange and confusing time. My best friend, a beautiful little girl with blonde hair, a delicate face, and big blue eyes, told us firmly one day in class, "If God didn't want us white people to conquer the Indians, he would not have let it happen." I was the only Indian person present, and I watched all the fifth graders nod their heavy heads so seriously.

I learned a great deal in the fifth grade. In fact, you might say that it was a turning point. I remembered that I once thought the whole world was Indian, was Otoe. I knew that these Indians the teacher and students were talking about were Grandpa Tom, Grandma Lena, Grandma Cora, my mother and father, Gi-su and me. I became aware that anytime Indians were discussed, it was always in reference to the past. I began to feel that in this school-world, I did not fit, though I performed very well in class. That disturbing feeling would eat away at me.

In my classes, I began to doubt the books, especially in history. Each year, I went through the history books before class started to see what the book said about me, about Indians. Often no mention was made at all. Other times, there was a whole paragraph describing how the people had been conquered, how we were a defeated people. The burning feeling started inside of me. Then I wondered what school was supposed to do for me. I studied the white and black children who were my classmates. They came from different worlds than I did. They would not, could not, understand the Pawnee and Otoe-Missouria in me. It became more apparent with the passing of each day.

There was a pale boy with watery blue eyes under thick glasses who tormented me in junior high school. He called me squaw. I didn't know what it meant exactly, but I did know the implications were not good. Inevitably there was a confrontation. It happened during speech class when the teacher asked a question. I raised my hand to reply.

Behind me, I heard him say to everyone else, "Let the squaw answer." Everyone heard. I stood up and turned toward him. The room became silent. Everyone looked at me. The teacher didn't move. I walked slowly to that boy, telling myself to be calm, and I lifted my right hand back as far as it would go and slapped him with the outrage of several years of torment. I recollect a red hand print over his freckles that stayed on his face for a few minutes.

That incident, too, marked another decisive point. I became more involved in things apart from the school. Often, I did not even go. I was not a poor student. I was never accused of being stupid. But nothing in school was worth the effort it took to sit there and endure it. This was a total transformation in attitude from what I first felt when I went to school. The gap simply widened each year. What did the subjects I was learning have to do with me? I was from Greasy Creek, I knew things abut life and reality that was not talked about in the books we studied, but who cared?

Then I became a "troublesome" student who wore "too much make-up," and associated with "the wrong people." I was very aware that neither grandmother of mine wore make-up, but those "wrong people" did not call me squaw. They simply didn't conform, as I refused to do. The classrooms were unbearable because they lied to me. What the teacher and book said was inconsistent with what I had known. I simply refused to believe in school, in anything.

Then I began to run away from home, but it was not my house I was trying to escape. It was from an ugly boy with freckles, and a counselor who attempted to advise me now and then. Her lectures began, "You're a smart girl, so I don't understand why you are not doing well. . . ." It was from this and much, much more that I wanted to flee.

As a child I was exposed to many Indian people who were alcoholics, but I remember one woman in particular. She had just undergone an operation where her stomach had been partially, or perhaps wholly, removed. She had a special little container inside of her to hold food. She did not take food through the mouth and was then on a liquid diet. Her husband had taken her out of the hospital for the week-end by special permission. Later, she sat in the midst of a crowd of people who were all drinking. She requested a drink from her husband as she lay on the bed. She could not sit for long periods. Her husband mixed her a drink and took it to her. I sat and played with my braids and tried to move closer when he lifted her blouse. Out of the purse, she produced a funnel. There was an opening in her stomach through which she was fed. He adjusted the funnel and poured the drink down it. I looked around at all the people there and asked myself, *Where did I fit in?*

We children saw handsome people become ugly and disfigured from drink. We heard of women raped in drunken stupor, heard of the children they had borne and never saw but once. We saw and heard of men and women kicked and beaten when they could not defend themselves, robbed and left for dead. We saw those things happen over and over, and always it was to the same people.

I hated it passionately, hated the people for being so vulnerable, so weak and defenseless. And yet, I also knew that those same characteristics that I hated in the people, were the ones that I possessed.

I continued to run away from home. The police or other authorities continued to return me there. I had a probation officer, a nice woman who regularly threatened to put me in a detention home for wayward girls. When things escalated to the point that I requested to be sent away, the probation officer began to reevaluate her strategy in counseling me. Finally, at the age of fifteen, I was involved in a car theft incident. The seriousness of it all hit me when about five police cars overtook the stolen vehicle and pulled us off the road. Potentially, I was a criminal. I felt as if I were drowning and didn't know how to swim.

As I looked around for help to pull myself out of the mess I had fallen into, I realized that no one was there. Grandpa Tom was long gone, Grandma Lena was ailing. There were other people in this world who were drowning around me, just as I was. They were older, but if they couldn't help themselves, I knew they couldn't help me. It was a selfish thought, a stark realization, and something to hold onto.

Gi-su, though younger than I, has often seemed older. She was always accepting of me and compassionate when no one else was. She was my only reality in an unreal and distorted world. It was a trying period, to have one person bear so much hate and anger. She shared it with me. And she was also there when a very strange thing occurred and touched us both.

One afternoon, Gi-su and I were walking down a road in our town discussing the things we had been up to lately—trouble. For some reason, a man in the distance caught our eyes. He came out of nowhere. He was an old brown man standing off our path. He clutched a cane in his hand and was immediately familiar to us. He was identical to Grandpa Tom, from the hat on his head to the tip of that cane. He looked very sternly at me, not at sister. He was angry, furious. It seemed he might lift his cane and use it if necessary. His eyes locked on mine. No words were spoken by him. There was no need. My heart began to thump loudly, and Gi-su stopped in her tracks. She whispered to me how much he resembled Grandpa, and that he seemed to very angry with me. Gi-su and I turned away from him and walked home, quietly, deep in thought.

When I was sixteen, I left Oklahoma for another boarding school. But this time, going to the boarding school was a choice that I made.

*   *   *

There are several Indian tribes in the United States who still choose to use their own tribal languages. There are a number of Indian people who have not yet made the transition to English. There are a few Indian people who have not learned English at all.

Such an example might be the Navajo. "My companion," for instance, designates the spouse. It is the preferred term which gives due respect in the company of men and women, but it is a new expression.

My companion is a Navajo. He is a member of the Maii Deeshigiizhinii Clan. He was "born for" the Tachinii Clan. This is to say that he is a member of the clan called Coyote Pass, or Jemez. It means his mother is of the Coyote Pass people. (The Navajos are a matrilineal society.) *Born for* identifies his father as a member of the Red Streak

Running Into The Water people: the Tachinii Clan. But he is a member of the Nood'i (Ute) Tachinii, not the true Tachinii.

It is said by the Navajos that they started with four clans "in the beginning." Today there are about seventy-six clans.

Relationship for the Navajo is determined by clan even today. When introducing oneself, clans follow names. The purpose is to establish clearly if one is related to another. This kinship introduction then allows one to be addressed in terms of clan relationship.

My husband's parents do not speak English, only Navajo. All their children spoke Navajo as their first language.

My husband's father was born between 1904 and 1908. He did not attend school but was brought up herding sheep and farming a few acres along the San Juan River. Traditional education was taught him by his uncle, his mother's older brother, who was a headman of the Cudei band of Navajos. His name was Sandoval, or Old Man Tall Grass. While my husband's father was still a child, he was taken to Sandoval to hear the old stories, chants, and songs from him. He was married twice, and his second marriage was to Nazba. She went to school for a short time and then became ill and was sent home. But she knew how to weave and herd sheep. The marriage between the two was an arrangement between Old Policeman and Short Hair Begay. Nazba was barely sixteen when she was married. Now the two have been married for about seventy years.

My husband was born in 1943. As a child, he knew Old Policeman and Short Hair Begay. Old Policeman lived in a hogan next to them at the base of the mountains where the family herded their flock of sheep. Old Policeman was then in poor health, an old man who was blind. Until Old Policeman's death, he was the undisputed ruler of the entire family, and my husband's father often performed chores for the old man. At the family farm along the San Juan River was where Short Hair Begay lived, and when my husband's folks were there clearing the land or harvesting their crop, the old man would often visit them. He would begin singing some distance away to announce his arrival.

One day when my husband was about seven or eight, a pastor from one of the churches in town came to visit his family, and four children left with the pastor to be put in the boarding school in town—three boys and a girl. The oldest boy was about twelve, the girl was a couple of years younger, then there was my husband, and the youngest brother was about six. Their mother had complained that the smallest boy was too young to be taken away, but it was to no avail, and he went to school anyway.

At school the boys were immediately separated from their sister without explanation. She was suddenly just gone. The boys were lined up and their names called, and that was the first time my husband heard his entire name. Then the boys were separated too, according to age groups. That day was a very disturbing one, and that night in the dormitory, my husband sneaked to his oldest brother's bed to discuss the events of the day. He found his younger brother already there with his older brother. The younger one was crying, and my husband crawled into bed with them and began to cry, too. They all worried about their sister, not knowing exactly where she was. Finally they slept. Before dawn, the oldest brother woke the younger two and sent them back to their own beds before everyone else got up.

My husband spoke only Navajo until then, and at the school his teachers and some of the staff spoke only English. On the first day of school, when the children were lined up and separated, the younger one began to cry when the oldest brother was separated from the others. One of the attendants noticed it. He cried more when the other brother, my husband, was also pulled out of the line. Harry says, "She (the attendant) came over and started to talk to him (brother). She rubbed his arms, and seemed to be asking if he was cold. She thought he was crying because he was cold."

There were other incidents when there was a communication problem. A time when my husband had to go to the bathroom and went to the teacher to explain this, but the teacher merely handed him a book to read. He took the book and thumbed through it, and then went to the teacher to try to explain his need again, whereupon the teacher took back the first book and replaced it with another. One of the Navajo housemothers was aware of the hard time the boys were having, and she talked to the children in Navajo: "I know you're having a hard time, but you need school. Our folks had harder times at Fort Sumner, and you have to get through this."

Those years were painful and lonely, and my husband still has difficulty talking about his experiences there. For all his school years he was housed in boarding schools away from his family. For all his school years he struggled to learn adequate English. In college he took remedial courses in English. He is still learning English but acknowledges that he will always think in Navajo.

His life has been one of moving from the mountains to the river and back again, following flocks of sheep and riding wagons through sagebrush and sand, and listening to his father and grandfathers sing through timeless journeys, nights and days. And when he was quite young, he took the things he saw and heard and began to render them in drawings and paintings. By the time he was in his late teens he was considered "a promising young Indian artist." This led him to Santa Fe.

The Institute of American Indian Art had just opened in Santa Fe and was to be an innovative institution in terms of Indian education. My husband attended the school in its first and second years of operation. I went in the second and third years. The school had recruited students from all over the United States who had an interest in fine and traditional arts. Over eighty tribes were represented there, but the common bond between all of us was that we were all Indian, Eskimo, or Aleut. Everyone there desired to create something from the substance of his own tribal identity and being. I quickly learned that several students had had school experiences such as mine, and that the students were excruciatingly sensitive to their environments. Many of the students came from urban areas, speaking English as their first language. A few were from the big cities where they had been raised all their lives, products of the Relocation Act when Indian families were moved to cities to assimilate, and these students had never been on a reservation. And then there were very traditional students who came from reservation areas and grew up speaking their own tongue first and English secondarily. It greatly impressed me that nearly all the Navajo students spoke Navajo to each other and thought of one another in kinship terms.

In talking with the other students, I learned that their tribes had nearly identical experiences as my own, and the students related accounts of their family histories that sounded like my own, too. I met people from tribes that I had often wondered about, such as the Seattle, the Seminole, and Cour d'lene. I heard some girls refuse to sleep on beds in the dorms because at home they did not have beds. They slept on the floor or under the beds. I learned that some tribes would absolutely not eat fish, and I sampled the dried fish that other tribes subsisted on entirely. I heard the stories of the Northwest Coast and met an ancestor of a chief whom I read about when I was a young girl.

We had access to Indian instructors at the school, something that was totally new to me. True, they were from tribes not my own, but they treated all the students respectfully, taking pains to draw from each a renewed self-respect, as well as respect for one another as Indian people. They accomplished this through the teaching of an art form of expression. Teachers such as Otellie Loloma, a Hopi potter and sculptor, quietly shaped clay and talked to each student in a soft voice, telling us about her struggle to obtain a meaningful education and at the same time not be forced to cut the ties with her people. Charles Loloma was another instructor who taught jewelry and painting, and he echoed Otellie's sentiments about their art and their people. Allan Houser, a painting instructor and sculptor, was a quiet man who joked softly with the students, not pressuring them to be anything but who they were, while he told stories of the Apache people, his own tribe. It was a wonderful experience to suddenly rediscover beautiful and valuable things again, and in the classroom!

The city of Santa Fe was also a beautiful place at that time. Its ancient past somehow melded with the present in a way that I hadn't seen previously. I learned from my Puebloan classmates that the Puebloan people had known of the Pawnees two or three centuries before I was born. So there on the streets of Santa Fe, where Pawnee slaves were once sold, everything I had been taught or known slowly began to fit together for me once more. As I watched the Pueblo dances, with the men and women's hair dragging on the ground as they danced, I suddenly remembered and felt to my bones just where it was and when

I was born. It was a thousand years ago, from a people's loins who came from the stars, and out of the water, and up out of the earth, and all the places they've been saying they were born since the beginning of time. There was no doubt anymore.

I spent about eight years in Santa Fe, coming to terms with myself and the world I lived in. After a year and a half at the Institute, I returned to Oklahoma for a brief visit and to get married.

My husband and I married out of our own tribes and into another. This is indicative of the times, and the implications of these marriages are numerous. Like many students at the Institute, some of whom traveled from across the United States to marry into another tribe, we experienced subtle changes of world view when we were allowed to intimately participate in another tribe's ceremonial life, or become part of their history via our future children. One of the reasons there is so much intermarriage now is the fact that many tribes are very small, and it is possible to be locked into a tribe through kinship. Since relationships are often counted to the fifth generation, there are a few tribes whose members are all related in a complex way. But the main influence of course is the amount of contact that we have these days with other tribes.

Our first son was born in 1966. When the baby was about a year old, we took him to Oklahoma to see Grandma Lena. It was the last time we visited her, and I was shaken by her defenselessness. She was an old Otoe woman standing alone at the edge of time. She had made the transition from young to old. It was not the same experience with Grandpa Tom, because when he grew old, he became young. Grandma Lena, who was always so strong, now sat so fragile before our youthful eyes. She sat in her wheelchair wearing the corn beads I had sent to her from New Mexico. She'd never been there and loved to talk about it. She said she could see the mesas and the mountains which I described to her in detail. She could see the Indians there, she said. (Indian people always seek each other out.) In reality, she could not see: She was totally blind. It was the first time that I witnessed her blindness. She sensed my discomfort and was embarrassed, but her embarrassment was not for herself, it was for me. She tried to put me at ease, and more or less apologized for letting herself grow old on me. Her hair was as white as the flour sacks she once used to make dresses for me. We sat for a while that day with her hand in mine, her eyes searching for the sound of my voice. We hardly talked, though there was much to be said. It just couldn't be said in words.

She took my baby boy and held him on her lap, caressing him and wishing aloud that she could lay eyes on him. It was satisfaction enough for her to lay hands on him. The "old folks" were always easy to please, easy to satisfy. This was one of their strengths and one of their weaknesses. She traced the baby's face, his eyes, mouth, and nose, and her hands went to his chubby hands and feet. Knowing that we would soon be parting for a very long time, I asked her something I'd never asked before. Who was she beside being "Grandma"?

When I asked, she looked toward my voice for a long time. Then she pulled herself up in that wheelchair until she was the tallest woman on earth. She straightened her skirts. She felt for the loose strands of hair which had fallen on her face, and pulled the hair sleek and knotted it swiftly at the neck. She smoothed down her hair, wiped her face clean with hands she blew on. Then she crossed her arms over her bosom. The picture was complete, haunting and fierce in its exaggeration. She visibly pushed away the years and gave me that proud, haughty image I knew, the one with dignity and grace. It was the image I wanted to see, and she felt it. She pursed her lips, stuck out her chin, and lifted her head like a bird. The sightless eyes blinked, and she became another person. Again she pursed her lips over toothless gums and looked down at the floor, not seeing anything with the cloudy eyes. But Grandma saw clearly a vision of the past that will never be seen again. It was then that she looked toward me and said with old pride, "My father was a chief." She smiled and looked thoughtful, stroking the baby in her arms. That was the final image she left me, and then illusive as a dream, she was gone.

She died in 1967 and was buried on the sloping hills near Red Rock, Oklahoma beside an old man who waited for her there through the years. Most of her family lay there on the hill as well.

In New Mexico, where we lived, Short Hair Begay often visited us, and other times we picked him up on the road as he walked from one place to another. Several times when I was alone at the house with the baby, the old man would come there. My baby boy would be running through the sagebrush, the top of his head barely visible in the tall brush. The old man would bring sweets—cakes or watermelons. He would sit on the floor with the baby and they would eat, while the old man carried on a long conversation with him in Navajo. The boy pleased him. Then, that old man passed away too.

In 1968 my second son was born, and he was carried to Oklahoma so that his Pawnee great-grandmother could see him, with his brother. She held the infant and the older boy in her arms, while she laughed gleefully over these new lives. Periodically, we visited her. It was on one such visit that another haunting thing happened. Grandma was at the nursing home, visiting with us, when my mother said to her, "Momma, we brought the photographs for you to see." I had several old tintype images of Captain Jim and old man Robert Taylor, which she had requested to see. Grandma looked quietly through the photographs, and my mother and I noticed that a tear fell here and there on the pictures. The pictures showed Captain Jim holding a huge fan, and Robert Taylor stood with some old Pawnee men. Grandma Cora looked at me, then to my mother, and said, "Oh my, I almost forgot. I almost forgot." She hugged the pictures to her chest and sobbed softly on my mother's shoulder. Mother said, "It's all right, Momma," as she held Grandma in her arms. And Grandma Cora answered, "No, it's not all right. I almost forgot. Do you understand?" She looked at my mother with a question in her eye, and my mother nodded, and they both wept together.

Finally "she went," as they say in Pawnee. When the Pawnees said it of Grandma, they pointed skyward with their lips. Grandma Cora was about ninety.

According to the Navajo people, or the Diné, as they call themselves, the world we live in today is the Fourth World. It is distinct from other worlds in that there are human beings here, or Earth Surface People. It is called "the glittering world." It marks a particular time. In the stories of the Four Worlds, it is not refuted that the most radical changes were foretold to occur in the Fourth World. That time is upon us. But everything is temporary.

The cycle from grandfather to grandchild is how we observe and measure the intangible time. The distance from Nebraska to Indian Territory, the distance from the First World to the Fourth World, and the distance from the four sacred mountains to Fort Sumner is then more comprehensible. Change and transition have often confronted us.

Indian Territory is not greatly different today than a century ago. Perhaps the humid land is a little more thick with people and is less naked than before. The nest in the hills where a few of us learned to fly exists only in our dreams. A massive lake and power plant sit on what was previously Otoe land. The lake will work for man, spouting out his precious energy for him. The old splintered house is beneath it. The hills that have brought forth life so many times are flooded. It was a natural bowl of quiet harmony. Now listen and hear the water churn. We knew the land in a dream before it had to work to justify its existence. It didn't do anything then but lay there naked in tall grasses under tornado winds. But that dream is drowned now—one sacrifice to, and for, time.

An old Otoe man took a lonesome stand against the blowing wind of time. His house was then burned to the ground before him. He cried the first handful of water that went into the lake. Then he went away. At least that is what everyone thinks and hopes he did.

Today this is where we are. Feel the wind in the hands of time, hear the wind blow.

It sings of a million people who have somehow survived since the dawn of each tribe: One tribe flourishes, while another one dies. Everyone is haunted by the songs of past winds. I am plagued by an old Otoe man who sang me Otoe songs. My mother is haunted by an old Pawnee woman who appeared and disappeared in a nightdream. She still hears the shuffle of moccasined feet that danced a memorable Ghost Dance in the night so long ago. Even those Ghost Dancers were haunted and danced to bring relief. My children are already haunted by the Yeibeichai, Fire Dancers, and the Horned Toad song. Yet we who live must sing of life in all the winds of time. We must take a stand in it and sing with the wind with all our might, or no one will know the song that somehow must be carried on.

I am an American Indian, but this simply does not say enough to satisfy the past, the present, or future. I am a Pawnee. I am an Otoe. My husband is a Navajo. And my children are all three.

Since my first day at school, I have heard and read that all the real Indians are gone: conquered, subdued, extinct, assimilated. And that those people of that descent are somehow less than their predecessors and are locked safely away from the mainstream society in time and cultural gaps they cannot escape. This innuendo is a burden on the grandchildren of those "real Indians" who are "gone." It is a weight on the spirit and its time it be lifted.

Each tribe that is recognized as such today has proved the right to collective identity by means of federal legislation for the last two centuries, and through ancient chants and songs for centuries prior to the American government, a recent development. The tribes have seen a thousand changes and yet remain who they are, and today in 1992, we are a people one million strong.

So we sing, have reason to sing of our peoples' lives and experiences. By our very existence, our birth—individual and collective, we cannot help but sing.

And changes to come? Grandma and Grandpa would say to these little children at our feet: "Everything changes, yet nothing changes but the holders of life. In great mystery, it is unending. That is the way of the Great Mystery. It knows not time."

Other titles from Firebrand Books include:

Artemis In Echo Park, Poetry by Eloise Klein Healy/$8.95

Beneath My Heart, Poetry by Janice Gould/$8.95

The Big Mama Stories by Shay Youngblood/$8.95

A Burst Of Light, Essays by Audre Lorde/$7.95

Cecile, Stories by Ruthann Robson/$8.95

Crime Against Nature, Poetry by Minnie Bruce Pratt/$8.95

Diamonds Are A Dyke's Best Friend by Yvonne Zipter/$9.95

Dykes To Watch Out For, Cartoons by Alison Bechdel/$6.95

Dykes To Watch Out For: The Sequel, Cartoons by Alison Bechdel/$8.95

Exile In The Promised Land, A Memoir by Marcia Freedman/$8.95

Eye Of A Hurricane, Stories by Ruthann Robson/$8.95

The Fires Of Bride, A Novel by Ellen Galford/$8.95

Food & Spirits, Stories by Beth Brant (*Degonwadonti*)/$8.95

Free Ride, A Novel by Marilyn Gayle/$9.95

A Gathering Of Spirit, A Collection by North American Indian Women edited by Beth Brant (*Degonwadonti*)/$10.95

Getting Home Alive by Aurora Levins Morales and Rosario Morales/$9.95

The Gilda Stories, A Novel by Jewelle Gomez/$9.95

Good Enough To Eat, A Novel by Lesléa Newman/$8.95

Humid Pitch, Narrative Poetry by Cheryl Clarke/$8.95

Jewish Women's Call For Peace edited by Rita Falbel, Irena Klepfisz, and Donna Nevel/$4.95

Jonestown & Other Madness, Poetry by Pat Parker/$7.95

Just Say Yes, A Novel by Judith McDaniel/$8.95

The Land Of Look Behind, Prose and Poetry by Michelle Cliff/$8.95

Legal Tender, A Mystery by Marion Foster/$9.95

Lesbian (Out)law, Survival Under the Rule of Law by Ruthann Robson /$9.95

A Letter To Harvey Milk, Short Stories by Lesléa Newman/$8.95

Letting In The Night, A Novel by Joan Lindau/$8.95

Living As A Lesbian, Poetry by Cheryl Clarke/$7.95

Making It, A Woman's Guide to Sex in the Age of AIDS by Cindy Patton and Janis Kelly/$4.95

Metamorphosis, Reflections On Recovery by Judith McDaniel/$7.95

Mohawk Trail by Beth Brant (*Degonwadonti*)/$7.95

Moll Cutpurse, A Novel by Ellen Galford/$7.95

The Monarchs Are Flying, A Novel by Marion Foster/$8.95

More Dykes To Watch Out For, Cartoons by Alison Bechdel/$7.95

(Continued)

Movement In Black, Poetry by Pat Parker/$8.95

My Mama's Dead Squirrel, Lesbian Essays on Southern Culture by Mab Segrest/$9.95

New, Improved! Dykes To Watch Out For, Cartoons by Alison Bechdel/$7.95

The Other Sappho, A Novel by Ellen Frye/$8.95

Out In The World, International Lesbian Organizing by Shelley Anderson /$4.95

Politics Of The Heart, A Lesbian Parenting Anthology edited by Sandra Pollack and Jeanne Vaughn/$12.95

Presenting...Sister NoBlues by Hattie Gossett/$8.95

Rebellion, Essays 1980-1991 by Minnie Bruce Pratt/$10.95

A Restricted Country by Joan Nestle/$8.95

Running Fiercely Toward A High Thin Sound, A Novel by Judith Katz/$9.95

Sacred Space by Geraldine Hatch Hanon/$9.95

Sanctuary, A Journey by Judith McDaniel/$7.95

Sans Souci, And Other Stories by Dionne Brand/$8.95

Scuttlebutt, A Novel by Jana Williams/$8.95

Shoulders, A Novel by Georgia Cotrell/$8.95

Simple Songs, Stories by Vickie Sears/$8.95

Speaking Dreams, Science Fiction by Severna Park/$9.95

The Sun Is Not Merciful, Short Stories by Anna Lee Walters/$8.95

Tender Warriors, A Novel by Rachel Guido deVries/$8.95

This Is About Incest by Margaret Randall/$8.95

The Threshing Floor, Short Stories by Barbara Burford/$7.95

Trash, Stories by Dorothy Allison/$8.95

We Say We Love Each Other, Poetry by Minnie Bruce Pratt/$8.95

The Women Who Hate Me, Poetry by Dorothy Allison/$8.95

Words To The Wise, A Writer's Guide to Feminist and Lesbian Periodicals & Publishers by Andrea Fleck Clardy/$4.95

The Worry Girl, Stories from a Childhood by Andrea Freud Loewenstein /$8.95

Yours In Struggle, Three Feminist Perspectives on Anti-Semitism and Racism by Elly Bulkin, Minnie Bruce Pratt, and Barbara Smith/$8.95

You can buy Firebrand titles at your bookstore, or order them directly from the publisher (141 The Commons, Ithaca, New York 14850, 607-272-0000).

Please include $2.00 shipping for the first book and $.50 for each additional book.

A free catalog is available on request.